Charles Eastman
Physician, Reformer, and Native American Leader

By Peter Anderson

Consultant: Jay Miller, Ph.D.
D'Arcy McNickle Center for the History of the American Indian
The Newberry Library
Chicago, Illinois

 CHILDRENS PRESS®
CHICAGO

PICTURE ACKNOWLEDGMENTS

The Bettmann Archive—page 54 (bottom)
Stuart Bratesman/Dartmouth College—pages 50 (2 photos),
    52 (left), 53 (top)
The Jones Library, Inc.—page 52 (right)
Minnesota Historical Society—pages 48, 49 (2 photos), 53 (bottom)
State Historical Society of North Dakota—page 8
North Wind Picture Archives—page 54 (top)
Sophia Smith Collection, Smith College—page 51 (2 photos)
YMCA of the USA Archives, University of Minnesota Libraries—
    pages 2, 88
Cover illustration by Len W. Meents

ACKNOWLEDGMENTS

All quotations used in this book come from: *From Deep Woods to
Civilization* by Charles Eastman (Boston: Little, Brown, and Company,
copyright 1917) and *Indian Boyhood* by Charles Eastman (New York:
McClure, Phillips and Company, copyright 1902).

Library of Congress Cataloging-in-Publication Data

Anderson, Peter, 1956-
    Charles Eastman: physician, reformer, and native American
leader/by Peter Anderson.
    p. cm.—(People of distinction biographies)

    Includes index.
    Summary: Follows the life of the Native American physician,
writer, and worker for his people's rights.
    ISBN 0-516-03278-X
    1. Eastman, Charles Alexander, 1858-1939—Juvenile literature.
2. Santee Indians—Biography—Juvenile literature. 3. Physicians—
United States—Biography—Juvenile literature. [1. Eastman,
Charles Alexander, 1858-1939. 2. Civil rights workers. 3. Santee
Indians—Biography. 4. Indians of North America—Biography.]
I. Title. II. Series.
E99.S22E1817   1992
973'.0497502—dc20
[B]   91-36654
                                                                    CIP
                                                                    AC
                                                                    Rev.

Table of Contents

Charles Eastman dressed in Sioux attire, a leather shirt and pants and feather headdress

Chapter 1

SPIRITS IN THE WOODS

One September day in 1873, a young Sioux hunter named Ohiyesa walked softly through the dark pine forests of southern Manitoba, Canada. Careful not to make any noise, he followed the trails left behind by deer and moose. He followed these trails through swamps and meadows and pine forests so thick he could hardly see the sky.

This was Ohiyesa's home. He had seen the colored shafts of the Northern Lights flashing through the night sky. He recognized the drumming sound that the partridge made, the lonely song of the whippoorwill, the strange laughing call of the loon. He knew where to find the wild cranberries and blueberries that grew in these woods. He had taken many fish from the shiny black waters of the rivers and streams.

Scarcely a day went by when he wasn't out hunting by himself. It was best that way. A young man gained strength from days spent alone in the wilderness, especially if he walked softly and paid attention. He might see the fresh tracks of a moose. He might hear the distant howl of a wolf. Maybe he would experience only the deep silence.

In this silence, Ohiyesa had been told, one could feel the mysterious force of creation. As he traveled through these forests, it was as though he began to absorb some of that mysterious force. His fear of the unknown had given way to a feeling that he belonged in these woods. He felt a sense of kinship with the animals around him.

Almost every day he would find wild game. And almost every day, he would bring meat back to camp. But not before offering a prayer. All forms of life—even trees and waterfalls—were filled with the spirit of creation and deserved respect. After Ohiyesa took a life, he held his pipe to the sky and sent his blessing up with the smoke to honor the animal's spirit.

Now, at the age of fifteen, Ohiyesa was hardly a boy anymore. He was already a skilled hunter. Soon, he would be a warrior. But none of his training, none of his skills, none of his experience had prepared him for what he was about to experience on that September day back in 1873.

As he walked out of the thick trees and into a large clearing, he sensed some commotion in his family's camp. Uncheedah, his grandmother, ran out to greet him. "Your father has come," she said.

Ohiyesa was stunned. How could this be? Many years ago, the whites had killed his father. Had his father now returned from the spirit land?

Chapter 2

THE RETURN OF MANY LIGHTNINGS

As far as Ohiyesa knew, his father, Many Lightnings, had been hanged by the whites eleven years earlier.

It had been a time of conflict between the Santee Sioux and the white settlers along the Mississippi River in southern Minnesota. On the reservation, poverty and disease had ravaged the Santees. Promised payment for Sioux lands had never been made. The tribe had split into factions. Frustrations were mounting. Tensions were high.

Then on August 17, 1862, four young Indians, no longer able to control their bitterness and anger, murdered five white settlers. This event, along with the conflicts that followed, was referred to by whites as the Sioux Uprising of 1862. After several battles, the violence came to an end in the Battle of Wood Lake where the United States army, under Colonel Henry Sibley, defeated a band of Santee Indians led by Little Crow. But as far as many of the white settlers in Minnesota were concerned, the Santee still needed to be punished. A court was set up, trials were held, and three hundred Indians were sentenced to be hanged.

Rather than accept the verdicts of the court, many of which were based on only shreds of evidence, Santee families fled to

Canada. In all the confusion, Ohiyesa was separated from his father and his two brothers. At the age of four, he was left with his uncle, Mysterious Medicine, and his grandmother, Uncheedah.

His father had never made it across the border. After he was sentenced to hang, Many Lightnings had tried to cross over into Canada but an informer turned him in. He was then taken back to Mankato, Minnesota, to await his execution.

Hearing protests about the mass hanging that was about to take place, President Abraham Lincoln stepped in. The trials, he felt, had been unfair; therefore, he issued a pardon for all but forty of the Santee who had been sentenced to die.

Still, the news was bad for Ohiyesa and his family. They received word that Many Lightnings was one of the Santee Sioux who had been hanged and buried in a mass grave near Mankato. Thus Ohiyesa, whose mother, Mary Nancy Eastman, had died during his birth, stayed with his uncle and grandmother.

What his family didn't know then was that Many Lightnings was still alive. After issuing his original pardon for all but forty of the Santee, Abraham Lincoln changed the death sentences for two more, one of whom was Many Lightnings. Instead of facing the gallows, Many Lightnings was sent to a federal prison in Davenport, Iowa, for three years.

There, Many Lightnings was exposed to the teachings of Christianity. After a while, he accepted the Christian faith and changed his name to Jacob Eastman, borrowing the last name from his late wife Mary. Mary had inherited the Eastman name from her father, Seth Eastman, a soldier in the United States army who later became a well-known artist.

After his release from prison in 1866, Jacob Eastman returned to the Santee reservation. In 1869, dissatisfied with the living conditions on the reservation, he and several other Santee families left to settle along the Big Sioux River. They applied to the government for homesteading land. When their requests were granted, these Sioux homesteaders formed the beginnings of the community that came to be known as Flandreau, South Dakota.

Once Jacob had established himself there, he wanted to find the rest of his family. Hearing that many of the Santee had settled farther north in Manitoba, he began his journey into the Canadian forests. Finally one morning in September of 1873, he found their camp.

When Ohiyesa came back from hunting later that day, Jacob Eastman was waiting for him. After thinking for so many years that his father was dead, Ohiyesa was stunned. Even after hearing Jacob's story, it was hard for Ohiyesa to believe that this was his father talking and not some voice from a distant spirit land.

But as strange as it was to see his father again after so many years, Ohiyesa was drawn to this man named Jacob Eastman. Still, he was bewildered when his father described the whites as kind and religious. Were these the people Ohiyesa had heard about? Mysterious Medicine, his uncle, had always portrayed the American whites as the enemy. While many of the Canadian whites seemed friendly to the Santee, the American whites had taken away Sioux land. And the American whites had hanged thirty-eight Santee men in Mankato, Minnesota. A Sioux warrior, his uncle had said, should never spare his enemy. It was the warrior's job to seek revenge.

Now his father was saying that it would be best for the Sioux to think of the American whites as brothers, that it would be best for them to accept the Christian religion, and that it would be best for Ohiyesa and the rest of the family to return with him to Flandreau.

Chapter 3

AN INDIAN BOYHOOD

The world that Ohiyesa knew was the world of the Sioux. After his long journey to Canada at the age of four, Uncheedah and Mysterious Medicine began to teach Ohiyesa the traditional ways of the hunter and the warrior.

Uncheedah, his first teacher, was a rugged, courageous woman, well respected for her knowledge and wisdom. After many days spent gathering roots and berries, she knew the forest well—so well, in fact, that many other Sioux women would come to her seeking knowledge about plants and herbs, especially those that made good medicine.

At times, it seemed as though her special relationship with nature had given her an almost supernatural awareness of the world around her. On one occasion, she had been uneasy about a campsite on the banks of the Assiniboine River. Even though it was after sundown, Uncheedah refused to pitch her tipi. This was not a good place, she told her family. They would have to camp somewhere else. Reluctantly, the others decided to move to a dark secluded place in the woods. Late that night, a family who had taken that camp by the river was killed by a roving band of warriors.

On another occasion, Uncheedah was alone in a camp with

her children when she noticed an unfamiliar footprint. Suspecting enemy warriors, she loaded her rifle and built a log fence around the tipi. Shortly after dark, a barking dog alerted her to five Ojibway warriors who were sneaking through the trees. Uncheedah opened fire and ran them off.

With her courage, her keen powers of observation, and her awareness of nature, Uncheedah made an ideal teacher for her young grandson. At once she introduced him to the rhythms of the natural world, putting him to bed when the birds quit singing and waking him in the morning when they began again at dawn. She taught him how to tell one bird's song from another.

As he got older, she took him along when she went out to gather plants. Only after a lengthy and careful inspection would she finally pick a plant. One day, her grandson asked how she knew which plants to use.

"The Great Mystery does not will us to find things too easily," she replied. "In that case everybody would be a medicine-giver ... [you] must learn that there are many secrets which the Great Mystery will disclose only to the most worthy."

The Great Mystery, she explained, was the spirit of creation present in all of life—in the stars, in the rivers, in the trees, in the birds. The more time a boy spent walking quietly through the forest by himself, she said, the more he would come to know the Great Mystery. She told Ohiyesa that nothing was more important than prayer and respect for the Great Mystery. That might mean giving prayers of thanks when the lives of animals were taken for food. It also might mean sacrificing a dearly loved possession. The only way that a boy could develop the power and strength he needed to become a warrior, she said, was to make a sacrifice to the Great Mystery.

It was Uncheedah who helped her grandson carry out such a sacrifice during the summer of his eighth year. "To-day you will make your first offering to [the Great Mystery]," she told her grandson. "You must give up one of your belongings— whichever is dearest to you."

The boy was puzzled. He wondered what would make the best gift. His bow and arrows? His bear-claw necklace? His otter-skin headdress? He mentioned these things to his grandmother. "Are these the things dearest to you?" Uncheedah demanded.

Again he thought hard. "I have nothing else as good as those things I have named," he told his grandmother, "unless it is my spotted pony; and I am sure the Great Mystery will not require a little boy to make him such a large gift." It had not occurred to him that there might be a gift even more precious than his pony.

"You must remember," Uncheedah said, "that in this offering, you will call upon him who looks at you from every creation. In the wind you hear him whisper to you. He gives his war-whoop in the thunder. He watches you by day with his eye, the sun; at night, he gazes upon your sleeping countenance through the moon. In short, it is the Mystery of Mysteries, who controls all things, to whom you must make your first offering."

"Grandmother, I will give up any of my possessions," he said, determined to live up to the challenge of becoming a warrior. "You may select what you think will be most pleasing to [the Great Mystery]." It was difficult for Uncheedah to tell him what needed to be done, but she knew, as she looked over at the black dog near the door of the tipi, what he loved most.

"You are a young brave," she said slowly. "I know ... your heart is strong and your courage is great. You will be pleased to give up the dearest thing you have for your first offering. You must give up Ohitika."

For a few moments, it seemed as though the boy hadn't heard what she had said. Then he answered her challenge, trying hard to hold back his tears.

"[Ohitika] will have to die!" said Ohiyesa, looking over at his dog with great sadness. "Let me tie together two of the prettiest tails of the squirrels that he and I killed this morning, to show to the Great Mystery what a hunter he has been." Ohiyesa tied the squirrel tails around the dog's neck. Then, like a warrior about to meet his death, he sang a dirge, or death song. Friends and family watched from a tipi admiring the young boy's courage. Uncheedah hated to see the boy's anguish but she knew it had to be, "Be brave, my Ohitika!" Ohiyesa said, as he brought the dog over to one of the older men who had agreed to carry out the sacrifice.

Then the boy followed his grandmother down a steep trail that dropped into a deep gorge. They walked down to the mouth of a huge cave. About fifty feet below them, the river rushed by. In front of them, a small stream flowed out of the cave and trickled down the side of the gorge, and a cool breeze blew. "It is the home of the Great Mystery," the boy thought to himself as his grandmother scattered offerings of tobacco. A woman named Wahchewin brought the dog's body down to the mouth of the cave. Uncheedah began her prayer.

"O Great Mystery, we hear thy voice in the rushing waters below us!" she said. "We hear thy whisper in the great oaks above! Our spirits are refreshed with thy breath from within this cave. O, hear our prayer! Behold this little boy and bless him! Make him a warrior and hunter as thou didst make his father and grandfather."

So it was that the young boy's life as a warrior and hunter officially began.

But Ohiyesa's training began much earlier. Sioux families emphasized the importance of bravery, a quality that Ohiyesa seemed to have even as a young boy. Once, hearing the loud cries of an invading Gros Ventre war party, he grabbed his bow and arrows and rushed out of the tipi, letting out his most ferocious war whoop. Uncheedah was able to grab him by the hair at the last minute, reminding him that young boys were not ready to be warriors.

Ohiyesa and the others like him were determined to test their courage in any way they could, but there was still much they had to learn. Imitating the actions of the older warriors and hunters, the young boys began to hone their skills in sports and other games like the mud and willow fight. In this make-believe battle, players carried large lumps of clay on the end of long springy willow wands. With as many as fifty or a hundred boys on a side, each with his own weapon, hard lumps of clay flew through the air at terrific speeds—as those who got hit knew all too well.

Another curious activity—all part of growing up for Ohiyesa and his friends—was the war against the wild bee. Imagining themselves as young warriors heading into battle, they would sneak up on the "enemy camp" (a bees' nest), hoping to destroy the enemy before the enemy fought back. Letting out their most blood-curdling war whoops, they trampled the beehive and ran off as fast as they could. Despite the usual bee stings, they would celebrate victory with a "scalp dance."

By his eighth year Ohiyesa had already experienced the adventures of hunting, but it wasn't until that summer that he encountered his first moose. While camping near the shores of a large lake, some of the older men had seen tracks. They went off in canoes, hoping to find moose on some nearby islands. Meanwhile, Ohiyesa was playing down by the lake. He saw what appeared to be the roots of a huge tree floating toward the shore. As it got closer, he suddenly realized that it was not a tree—but a moose swimming for shore.

Hiding in some nearby brush, he took out one of his sharpest arrows as the moose emerged from the lake. As the long-legged moose shook himself off, Ohiyesa stood up, let out a great war whoop, and fired his arrow. The moose didn't seem to mind the arrow, but he was frightened by the noise and was soon out of sight. Ohiyesa figured he must have been the smallest hunter ever to have an arrow carried away by a moose.

Like Uncheedah, Mysterious Medicine advised Ohiyesa to be silent and observant in the forest. Each morning he would tell the young hunter to look closely at the world, and each evening he would quiz Ohiyesa about the plants and animals he had seen. "In hunting," Mysterious Medicine told him, "you will be guided by the animals you seek." Mysterious Medicine taught him about their habits: how the moose like swampy lowlands between lakes or mountains, how the deer often make two big loops before settling into a hiding place, that the best time for taking lots of fish is early in the morning when they are spawning.

Under Mysterious Medicine's guidance, Ohiyesa began to develop the discipline required of a Sioux warrior. All boys were expected to endure great hardships without complaining. They were expected to be able to travel for several days without food or water. Mysterious Medicine made sure that Ohiyesa had the proper training to develop such endurance. Sometimes he would waken his nephew early in the morning and challenge him to fast all day. They would blacken their faces with charcoal so that everyone knew they were fasting. Then, refusing to give in to offers of food from the other boys in camp, Ohiyesa would have to fast until the sunset.

On other occasions, Mysterious Medicine would awaken Ohiyesa with a war whoop, sometimes with rifle shots and bloodcurdling screams. Ohiyesa was expected to leap up immediately. If he was startled or sleepy, Mysterious Medicine would remind him that a warrior needed to be ready at all times if he wanted to keep his scalp.

When they were out camping in unknown territory together, Mysterious Medicine would send the boy out for water long after dark. As Ohiyesa wandered through the pitch-black forest, every owl hoot sounded like an enemy warrior. Every cracking twig made him think of bears. Still, he pushed on through the woods until he found water. Then he would struggle back to camp in the darkness. There his uncle would greet him. "You are a thorough warrior," he would say, as he emptied the water from the bucket. Then he would order Ohiyesa to fill the bucket again. Ohiyesa would walk once again through the dark forest knowing that it was all part of the warrior's training.

By the time he was fifteen years old, Ohiyesa was well prepared for life in the dark Canadian forests. When he received a flintlock rifle from Mysterious Medicine, it seemed to the boy that his time had come. Now, he was ready to follow in the tradition of the great hunters and warriors before him.

Chapter 4

INTO THE WHITE WORLD

Ohiyesa's father had different plans for his son. Before his imprisonment, Jacob admitted, the Sioux way of life had been best. But now, with so many whites coming into the territory, it was useless to resist change. The whites were powerful and so was their God. The sooner Indians realized that and gave up the old ways, the better.

For that reason he had taken a new name, a white person's name. For that reason, too, Jacob Eastman wanted to take his son back to Minnesota. There Ohiyesa would have the opportunity to enter an entirely different world—a world of farms and villages where he would be able to attend the churches and mission schools set up by whites. In Flandreau, there would be other Sioux people—some thirty families—who had settled on homesteads and who had come to accept the Christian faith.

Despite his brother's words, Mysterious Medicine was still suspicious of the American whites and their way of life. Ohiyesa's uncle had come to love the Canadian forests. He was unwilling to give up the freedom of the hunter's life. But Ohiyesa had little choice.

Despite his reluctance to give up the places and the people

he knew and despite some lingering questions, he felt an obligation to his father. True, he had grown up thinking that whites were the enemy, but his father described them as religious and friendly. He had to accept his father's word. If Jacob wanted him to give up the warrior's path, Ohiyesa would have to honor his father's wishes.

But it all seemed so strange. He might never see his friends again. And how difficult it was to say good-bye to Mysterious Medicine, his beloved uncle. It was as if a part of him would have to die so that he could join his father on this journey into the white world.

At least Uncheedah was coming. Despite her reluctance about giving up the old ways, she wanted to return to Minnesota where she had spent much of her life. But the land they returned to hardly seemed like the land she had known. Where there had once been only forests, now there were many more farms and homesteads. And it was on one such homestead, on the edge of a narrow strip of trees overlooking the Big Sioux River, that Uncheedah and Ohiyesa would make their new home.

Instead of thick woods filled with deer and moose, Jacob Eastman's cabin was surrounded by fields of wheat, corn, and potatoes. For Ohiyesa, who was used to the forests of Manitoba, all that flat land stretching out to such a long horizon made the world seem empty.

Only a month had passed and already his life had become very different. Even his name had been changed. Throughout their journey south, Ohiyesa's father had been reading from the Bible and singing Christian hymns. Hoping his boy would learn to believe in the Christian God, Jacob arranged for a proper baptism. He chose the names Charles and Alexander out of a minister's book.

Ohiyesa had become Charles Alexander Eastman. His name had been changed but the rest of him hadn't. He respected his father's religious faith and appreciated his kindness, but Charles was still a hunter and a warrior at heart. Little wonder that he had a hard time fitting in at the mission school in Flandreau. When he went to the schoolhouse, forty other students, most of them younger, stared at him as he walked up the hill. Even though most of them were Sioux, they were dressed like the whites and their hair was cut short. To Charles, they looked strange. To them, he seemed wild and mysterious.

It soon became obvious that Charles had little in common with his schoolmates, especially when it came to language. Without knowing any English, he had no idea what his teacher was saying. Numbers and letters written on a blackboard meant nothing. He couldn't even follow the simplest of his teacher's instructions—much to the amusement of the other students who laughed at him and teased him until he couldn't take it anymore.

Rising silently from his desk, he walked out the door. This was not the place for him. Learning to do things differently was, for him, like a buffalo learning how to make a beaver's den. And how would this school make him any braver? As he rode off on his pony, he considered returning to Canada to live with his uncle. If his father wanted to live with whites, he could do so. For Charles, it could never work. He would have to tell his father that he couldn't stay.

But Jacob Eastman convinced him otherwise. He understood his son's grief—no one enjoyed being ridiculed—but he encouraged Charles to be strong and to think of himself as a warrior on a new trail. The path to knowledge, he told his son, would be difficult and there would be great challenges, but there also would be rewards. Ohiyesa had become a hunter and a warrior. In the same way, his father told him, Charles Alexander Eastman would learn the ways of the white world.

So Charles decided to return to the mission school. He even cut his hair short and wore the clothes that had looked so strange on the other students that first day. But understanding his English-speaking teachers was a difficult task. And when he did, he wondered what their book talk had to do with anything important like hunting or even planting corn.

Uncheedah wondered too. She was concerned that her grandson was leaving behind the traditions that she had taught him. To make matters even more confusing for young Charles, Uncheedah and his father often argued.

"This is not a true life. It is a sham," she told Jacob. "I cannot bear to see my boy live a made-up life."

"There is no going back," Jacob Eastman told her. "Besides,

one would be like a hobbled pony without learning to live like those among whom we must live."

"I say it is against our religion to change the customs that have been practiced by our people ... " Uncheedah argued. "Many of the school-children have died, you have told me. It is not strange. You have offended Him [the Great Mystery], because you have made these children change the ways he has given us."

"The white man has a well-grounded religion and teaches his children the same virtues that our people taught to theirs," Jacob told her. "The Great Mystery has shown to the red and white man alike the good and evil."

While he saw common threads in the ribbons of the white and Indian people, Jacob Eastman believed that the whites had accumulated more wisdom because they had written down their ideas. Knowledge of these writings, he believed, was necessary for the Indian to live side by side with the whites. If there were sacrifices to be made in order to attain that knowledge, then they should be made.

"The way of knowledge," he told his son, "is like our old way in hunting. You begin with a mere trail—a footprint. If you follow that faithfully, it may lead you to a clearer trail—a track—a road. Later on there will be many tracks, crossing and diverging from the other. Then you must be careful, for success lies in the choice of the right road."

But Charles still wasn't sure that the road he had chosen

was the right one. If he would displease the Great Mystery as his grandmother suggested, it couldn't be right. After all, what was more important than expressing one's respect for the Creator?

Still, he couldn't ignore his father's strong opinions. It was true that the whites had great knowledge and power, there was no question about that. Charles had seen the guns and gunpowder, the steel knives and hatchets, and he had heard of the great railroads. And besides, there were more and more white settlers coming into this territory all the time. Maybe it would be best to learn their ways.

But it was still confusing. Two of the people that he loved most had such different ideas. How could he choose between them? Seeking the comfort of the Great Mystery, he wandered out across the fields and farther into the trees, and he walked through the cool shady groves, deeper and deeper, until the trees covered most of the sky.

Chapter 5

A HIGHER CALLING

When Charles returned from the forest, his heart was strong, his thoughts clear. As a boy, when he saw a track he did not know, he would follow it until an animal revealed itself. By following their tracks, he had come to understand the animals' habits and, in this way, he became a hunter. Now, at the age of sixteen, he was ready to hunt new knowledge.

In the fall of 1874, after one year at the mission school in Flandreau, he was sent to the Santee Normal School in Santee, Nebraska. "Remember, my boy," his father said, "it is the same as if I sent you on your first war-path. I shall expect you to conquer."

Those were words that stayed with young Charles as he paused to listen to the music of a waterfall on his way to Santee. The sound of rushing water called him back once again to the woods of his childhood. Was he really making the right choice? Wouldn't he be better off to point his pony to the north and return to the Canadian woods? Then he thought of his father—how disappointed he would be if his son were to abandon his chosen trail.

So he continued out across the empty prairie toward the

Santee School. Late that afternoon, as he dropped down into a valley and walked toward a small stream, he noticed a sod house. There he was met by a bearded white man, the first person he had seen all day.

Charles held out the coins his father had given him, offering with hand signals to trade them for food. The man invited him in for dinner. He was greeted by the man's wife and five children, whose curious eyes followed him as he took his place at their table. Had he not been so hungry, he never would have stayed. Even after his year at the school in Flandreau, Charles shied away from strangers.

When the man smashed the butt of his knife against the table, Charles jumped up and almost ran out the door. Then he realized that this was the man's way of getting the family's attention. His wife and children became silent. Then the man said grace.

After dinner Charles once again offered his money, but the man only smiled and shook his head, inviting him to join the family in the parlor. Charles politely declined. It was hard for him to feel comfortable in such strange surroundings—better just to stay outside by the stream where he felt more at home.

But when he heard the strange music drifting out over the field, his curiosity led him back to the house. How did someone put sound in a box, he wondered, as he watched the woman step on a pedal and press on the black and white keys of an organ? He listened to their hymns while the sky grew dark.

The next day, he said his farewells to the family. These were kind people, he thought to himself, as he continued his journey to the west. Maybe there was goodness in the white world after all.

For three days he rode, until he reached the hills along the Missouri River. Before him a long slope dropped off to the river bottom. This slope was covered, as far as he could see, with farmhouses and fields. This was the white people's world at its best, Charles thought. He admired these homes and the lush fields that surrounded them.

Continuing across the Missouri, Charles finally arrived at Santee Normal where he was welcomed by his brother John, an assistant teacher at the school. When other family members fled to Canada after the Santee uprising, John had stayed behind with his father. Already well schooled and knowledgeable about the world he lived in, he helped his younger brother get acquainted with these new surroundings.

Doctor Alfred Riggs, the superintendent of the school, impressed Charles with his friendliness and his knowledge of the Sioux language. Sometimes, out of shyness, Charles would wander off into the nearby woods to be alone, but gradually, with support from Doctor Riggs, letters from his father, and the affection of his older brother, he found the strength to make new friends. There were, after all, other Sioux boys who were facing some of the same struggles when it came to learning a new language. When Charles stumbled over simple three-letter words in class, he at least knew that his friends

Kite and Eagle-Crane were struggling with him.

As his English improved, he began to understand the long prayers that Doctor Riggs read in the chapel. What he didn't understand was this idea of praying in a church. As far as Charles was concerned, the best way to pray was out in the wilderness—alone. How could anyone show respect for the Great Mystery inside a building filled with young boys and girls?

Had it not been for Doctor Riggs, Charles might never have come to accept the Christian way of prayer—not to mention some of their other strange customs. But Charles admired the superintendent and trusted him as a teacher. The fact that Doctor Riggs thought it was all right to pray in this way eventually convinced Charles that it was all right.

Doctor Riggs also had great respect for Charles. Not only was Charles willing to help out with chores around the school, but he also studied harder than most of his fellow students. By the end of his second year at Santee, Charles had caught up with students who had been in school several years longer than he had. Soon he was able to translate every word from his English books into his native tongue. Seeing Charles's accomplishments, Doctor Riggs arranged for a scholarship so that Charles could continue his education at Beloit College in Wisconsin.

Leaving behind his brother and Doctor Riggs would be difficult. Charles was uneasy about the idea of traveling alone to a college where he knew no one. Still, he eagerly accepted. Then, on the evening before his departure, sad news came from Flandreau. After a short sickness his father had died.

That night, he thought long and hard about his father. He thought of their meeting in Canada. He could almost hear Jacob's hymns and prayers on the journey south to Minnesota. He pictured his father as he had last seen him, young and strong and working hard on his farm in Flandreau. How could it be that he was gone so suddenly? He recalled, with gratitude, his father's many words of encouragement. "My son," Jacob once had written him in a letter, "I believe that an Indian can learn all that is in the books of the white man." As he gathered his belongings for the trip to Beloit, Charles vowed to do just that.

The next day, he boarded a train for the first time in his life. Awed by the power of the fiery locomotive, he gazed out across the rolling hills. As the train left Yankton, South Dakota, his thoughts were full of questions. Where would this new trail lead him? Would he be able to keep up with the work at the college?

As the train rumbled east, the towns became bigger and grew closer together. Because he had been warned by his brother and other friends about pickpockets and other dangers of the bigger towns and cities, Charles was hesitant to wander too far from the station while waiting to change trains; however, he did venture out to a nearby restaurant. The fast-talking waitress was hard to understand, so Charles simply nodded his head agreeing to whatever she said, and mistakenly he ordered most of the menu.

On the second day of his railroad adventure, Charles arrived in Beloit. There, he was greeted by Doctor Chapin, the president of the college. Later, he was shown to his room in one of the campus dormitories.

It was September of 1876. Several months earlier, General George Armstrong Custer and his troops had been defeated in a battle with the Sioux at Little Bighorn. Later, Charles would learn that his two uncles had been involved in that famous battle—a conflict that had angered many white people.

When Charles arrived in Beloit, word got around that there was a Sioux Indian student attending the college. Rumors spread quickly. "We have Sitting Bull's nephew here," he heard a voice shout from a dorm window that first day, "and he'll likely have your scalp before morning." An article in the local paper claimed that Sitting Bull had sent Charles as a representative to learn about the whites' way of life. When Charles walked around downtown, gangs of young white boys trailed behind him, imitating Indian war whoops.

Somehow, in the midst of all the commotion, Charles managed to study. At Santee he had been able to translate written English into his native tongue. Now he had to learn to *speak* with whites. At times, he felt like a deaf person as he tried to understand the fast, fluent words of his teachers and the other students. Sometimes by watching their facial expressions, he came to understand them and, after a while, the words began to sound familiar. Not only did he polish his English skills, but he also learned more in the areas of geography, history, and mathematics. To keep himself in good shape physically he exercised for three hours each day, a routine that prepared him well for a summer of farm work.

Finding a job proved to be another kind of challenge. As soon as school let out for the summer, Charles traveled south with a letter from Doctor Chapin, hoping to find work. Still somewhat shy, he found it difficult to approach strangers; nevertheless, he stopped at the first farm he came to and knocked on the door. A young girl answered the door and asked him to wait. Finally, the farmer came in from his field and eyed Charles suspiciously.

"Well, young man, what do you want?"

"I am a student of Beloit College," said Charles, "and I am looking for work."

"What tribe do you belong to?" asked the farmer, still suspicious.

"I am Sioux," Charles replied.

"Get off ... my farm," the farmer snapped, "I had a cousin killed by your people only last summer."

Shaken and discouraged, Charles walked on. At the next farm he knocked on the door and immediately presented his letter from the college. This time a more sympathetic farmer offered him a job that he gratefully accepted. After several months in the fields, Charles returned to Beloit stronger and more confident—and with some extra money to show for his labors.

For three years, Charles studied at Beloit. Then, Doctor Riggs, his trusted mentor, arranged for him to continue studying at Knox College in Tennessee with the aid of a government scholarship. There, Charles began to wonder about his future occupation. He had proven himself in school, but now it was time to apply his knowledge. How could he contribute? Even though he had learned a great deal, he still hadn't been trained in any particular skill. It was this kind of training that he now yearned for. And it was this kind of training that he found at Dartmouth College and Boston University.

Once again, Doctor Riggs helped him to obtain a scholarship. This time it enabled him to attend Dartmouth, a well-respected college in Hanover, New Hampshire, which was originally established as a school for Indians. There, Charles decided that he would become a doctor. In the fall of 1883, he began an ambitious course of study that included classes in language, science, and social studies. But even before he went to his first class, he had become well known around campus.

On the evening before classes were to begin, his classmates, hearing that they had a Sioux Indian in their ranks, elected him captain of the freshman football team. A Sioux warrior would be a tough leader, they reasoned—not to mention the fact that he would scare all the sophomores off the football field.

As if he wasn't getting enough attention already, Charles soon found himself in the pages of a Boston newspaper. A reporter wrote with great amusement about the Sioux football captain who tried to "scalp" one of the professors. It seems Charles had mistakenly tackled a philosophy professor who had walked by during a game against the sophomores.

Despite all the attention, Charles remained humble and good-natured, and he continued to shine in the classroom and on the athletic field. He played baseball and tennis. He became an accomplished boxer. And for three years he held the school record for long-distance running.

In June of 1887, Charles was graduated from Dartmouth with honors. He was ready, he thought, to return to the reservation where he hoped to work as a medical missionary. But his supporters, among them Mr. and Mrs. Frank Wood, believed he should continue his medical training. Mr. and Mrs. Wood, who had become acquainted with Charles through Doctor Riggs, admired this young Indian man. They were determined not to let anything get in the way of his education. When Charles had money needs, they took care of them or found friends who could. They also provided emotional support when Charles needed it, and acquainted him with the social customs—everything from good manners to proper dress— of East Coast society.

Mr. and Mrs. Wood and their friends were sympathetic to the plight of the many American Indians who had been displaced from their homelands and their traditions. To them, Charles offered hope. He was proof that with the proper education and support an Indian could succeed in the white world.

With their help, Charles received another scholarship to Boston University. There, he spent three years learning the skills he would need to practice medicine. He had already earned the gifts of knowledge; now, he could put it to use working as an intern on the south side of Boston. Someday he hoped to bring these skills home to the people of the Sioux nation.

Chapter 6

THE SIOUX DOCTOR

In the middle of a dust storm that swept across the South Dakota prairie in November of 1890, Charles Eastman arrived at the Pine Ridge Agency on the Sioux reservation. He had taken the job of government doctor at this desolate outpost. The prairie wind blew through the cracks of the rundown shack that would be his new home. Inside, the furnishings—a wood stove, a desk, a couple of chairs—were covered with Dakota sand. There were no carpets on the floor, no curtains on the windows. He didn't even have a bed.

His new surroundings couldn't have been more different from the college campuses of New England but that didn't matter. What mattered was that he felt at home with these people and *that*, Charles believed, was absolutely necessary for a doctor to have any success on the reservation. Some government doctors who felt superior to their patients tried to impress the Indians with their knowledge, but this was not the way as far as Charles was concerned. Gaining the confidence of the Sioux people would require humility and compassion. His approach would be one of sympathy and kindness.

The next morning, his first official day as the agency physician, he boarded up a small window on the side of his shack.

He wasn't simply going to dole out medicine through the window like the previous doctor had done. The agency doctor's role, as Charles understood it, was more than just prescribing drugs. He intended to examine his patients thoroughly before giving them any medicine, but he soon found out that would be difficult.

His first day on the job was also the first day of the "Big Issue." During the Big Issue thousands of Sioux people, who lived in scattered camps and homes throughout the region, came into the government agency for a weekly ration of food and supplies. It was the only way they could survive. Most of their hunting grounds had been confiscated, the buffalo herds had been killed, and the reservation land was poor for farming.

While a steady stream of Sioux people flowed into the agency — some riding lumber wagons, some on horseback, and others who had come many miles on foot — Charles did his best to keep up with the patients that came to his door. Although many of his Indian patients came only to request certain medicines, Charles tried to offer them more. They were surprised when he asked about their ailments. They were even more surprised that he spoke their language. When he had any time at all between patients, he tried to keep written records. Sometimes he would even visit patients in their camps.

Nevertheless, he quickly understood why the other doctors had simply resigned themselves to passing out medicine. It was impossible to give thorough treatment to all the patients that came to his door. To make matters worse, numerous people came to visit him less for reasons of health and more out of curiosity—they wanted to see this "Indian white doctor."

During the first week and a half he rarely had time to rest— maybe a couple hours of sleep each night at best. He began to wonder why the United States government provided only one doctor for six thousand Sioux people.

And if the sheer numbers of patients weren't enough to push a doctor to the limits, there were other challenges. Many of the Sioux people Charles treated were suspicious of his medical practice. Plaster casts for broken bones seemed strange to them. Patients usually removed them shortly after leaving the doctor's office. Any kind of surgery was a frightening thought and amputations, no matter how badly needed, were out of the question.

It was with cases like Three Stars' wife that Charles gradually won their confidence. Three Stars, one of the Sioux chiefs who had converted to the Christian religion and was more open to their medicine as well, came in one day with his wife who had dislocated her shoulder.

"Can you help her?" he asked.

"Yes," Charles said, "but I must first put her to sleep. You should have brought her to me last night, when it first happened," he added, "and then that would not have been necessary." Charles gave her an anesthetic which made her lose consciousness. Then he jerked the arm back into its socket. As

Three Stars' wife came to, she was laughing—much to the amusement of the other Indians standing nearby. To them, this medicine was miraculous. From then on, it wasn't unusual for someone in pain to request the medicine that "made the wife of Three Stars laugh."

Shortly after this incident, another successful treatment helped convince the Sioux that Charles had powerful medicine. A man whose leg had been totally crushed came to Charles seeking help. Charles convinced the man that only amputation could save him. Reluctantly, the patient agreed to the surgery. As a result of the amputation, he not only recovered his health but was soon able to walk on an artificial leg.

Still there were those who preferred the treatments of the traditional Sioux medicine men. These medicine men, Charles had been told, were opposed to modern medicine and would do all they could to discourage their patients from seeking it out. Nevertheless, Charles approached them in an open and friendly manner.

On one occasion, the parents of a sick child each had their own ideas about the best way to treat the illness. The mother sent for the medicine man. The father asked for Charles. When Charles arrived, the medicine man was already at the sick child's bedside.

"Brother," he said to the medicine man, "I am glad you got here first. I had a long way to come, and the children need immediate attention."

"I think so too," said the medicine man, "but now that you are here, I will withdraw."

"Why so?" asked Charles. "Surely two doctors should be better than one." Before beginning treatment, Charles offered to join the medicine man in a sweat lodge—a domelike hut where Sioux people offered prayers and songs to the Great Mystery. Hot rocks were taken from a fire and placed on the floor of the hut. Together in the intense heat, Charles and the medicine man sang and said prayers. In this way they found a common bond and were able to work together. The medicine man later became one of Charles's friends and occasionally borrowed some of his medicine.

As Charles earned the trust of his fellow Sioux, they came to confide in him. It wasn't unusual for parents to approach him in order to get their children excused from school. Most of the children on the reservation attended a large boarding school at that time and were allowed to visit their parents only on days when the government issued supplies and rations. When it was time for them to return to school, Charles had many lonely mothers and homesick children knocking on his door. Mothers would plead with him to provide an excuse so that they could keep their children for an extra day. Even though Charles believed in the cause of education, which he gently tried to convey to these families, there were times, especially when talkative grandmothers pleaded the case too, that he would provide them with a written excuse.

Before long, Charles had made many friends among the Sioux; one of these was Captain Sword, chief of the Indian police force at the agency. It was Captain Sword who first told Charles about a new religion known as the Ghost Dance that seemed to be catching on with members of the tribe.

The Ghost Dance religion had originated with a Paiute medicine man named Wovoka who lived in Nevada. Wovoka believed that this dance—a slow, shuffling, circle dance—would empower the Indian people. It would enable them to return to the way of life they had known before the whites came. Their dead ancestors would return. Their lands would once again be wild and full of game.

These ideas came during times of great suffering for the Sioux people. In 1888, herds of their cattle were killed by disease. In 1889, their crops failed. Epidemics swept through the reservation. As if all of these natural hardships hadn't been bad enough, it seemed as though the white government was working against the tribe again. Later that year, the United States Congress passed a law that divided the Sioux territory into six smaller reservations. The tribe lost land and they lost a sense of unity.

Maybe the Ghost Dance was their only hope. Some of the Sioux leaders saw it as a way to rally their people together to protest the poor treatment they were receiving from the white government. Government officials were concerned and said that the Ghost Dance must stop. It was this aspect of the new religion that concerned Captain Sword.

"My friend," he told Charles, "our reservation has been free from this new teaching until the last few weeks. Quite lately this ghost dance was introduced ... [and] the Great Father at Washington [the U.S. government] wishes it stopped. I fear the people will not stop. I fear trouble." Shortly after the visit from Captain Sword, the government agent at Pine Ridge expressed similar concerns to Charles. The Ghost Dance was creating difficulties, he said. The Sioux were disobeying government orders and it might be necessary to call in army troops. Charles couldn't help but feel the tension mounting, but for a while anyway, his thoughts were elsewhere.

It was at a Pine Ridge tea party held in honor of a visiting missionary that Charles met an intriguing woman. Raised on an isolated farm in western Massachusetts, Elaine Goodale had been educated at home by her parents. Encouraged to live a life of service, she had decided to become a teacher and, at the age of twenty, had joined the staff at the Hampton Normal and Agricultural Institute in Virginia.

Following the United States military conquest of the Plains Indian tribes in the 1870s, there was a need to provide education for Indians now forced to live in a world dominated by whites. Hampton was among the schools that tried to fill that need. Elaine's first class assignment involved teaching English to Indian men. Preparing Indians for white society, she decided, would be the best way for her to serve society. She took it upon herself to see how Indians were being educated elsewhere around the country.

While on a tour of the Sioux reservation, she saw some of the Indian schools that had been set up by the Episcopal church. On that same tour she also noticed an abandoned schoolhouse on the White River. Later, she decided it was her mission to reopen that school.

Two years after she began teaching at Hampton, Elaine and a friend reopened that schoolhouse near the Brule Agency and were soon teaching up to fifty children between the ages of six and sixteen. She intended to introduce these children to basic skills like reading, writing, and mathematics. She also wanted to teach her values. Adopting these values, she believed, would enable them to live more productive lives.

By the time Charles met Elaine at that tea party in Pine Ridge, she had become the supervisor for all the Indian schools in Nebraska and the Dakotas, an impressive job for a twenty-two year old, he thought. He also had read some of her articles on Indian education and was impressed with her sincere desire to help the Indian people. But what really impressed Charles was her charm and personality. He was attracted to her, as she was to him, and hoped that they would see each other again soon.

But it was time for another Big Issue, and Charles was once again overwhelmed with patients and visitors. Among the visitors was Captain Sword who again expressed his concern about the Ghost Dance. He told Charles that the government agent had told all his employees on other parts of the reservation to bring their families into the agency immediately. "This means that something is going to happen," Sword said. "I have heard that he will send for soldiers to come here to stop the Ghost Dance. If so, there will be trouble."

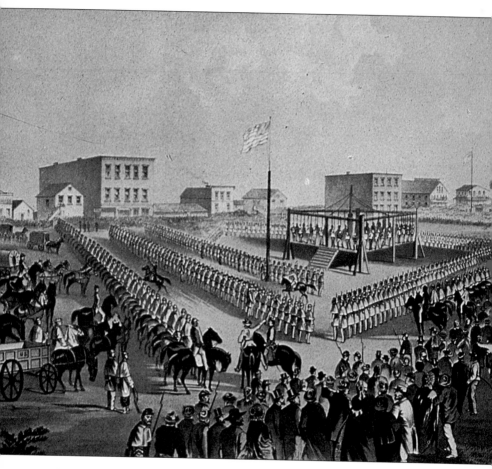

An engraving showing the mass hanging of the thirty-eight Sioux Indians at Mankato, Minnesota, in 1862. Charles's father, Many Lightnings, was one of the last to be pardoned by President Abraham Lincoln.

Charles entered the Santee Normal School in 1874.
Above: The faculty of Santee Normal School and Reverend
Riggs and his family stand in front of Reverend Riggs' house.
Below: Pupils working in the garden at the school

Charles is part of the groups in these Dartmouth class photos taken in 1887. He is seated in the center front in both photos.

Above: Charles Eastman and Elaine Goodale before
their marriage in 1891
Below: The first Teachers' Institute in Indian Service was
called by Elaine Goodale in 1890. She is standing on the right.

Charles Eastman

Elaine Goodale Eastman

Above: In 1927 Charles dressed in native clothing at his
fortieth class reunion at Dartmouth.
Below: John Eastman, Charles's brother

Above: A photograph of Sitting Bull
Below: The camp of Sitting Bull in
Standing Rock, North Dakota

Chapter 7

CAUGHT BETWEEN TWO WORLDS

One morning in November of 1890, Charles noticed a cloud of dust on the eastern horizon. As the sun rose above the pine-covered ridges, he could see that the cloud was getting closer. The Ninth Division of the U.S. Cavalry, he soon found out, was on its way.

As the news spread, women and children from nearby Sioux camps, fearing an attack, came into the agency seeking refuge. Charles tried to reassure them. The soldiers were only coming to keep the peace, he told them; but, down deep, he was concerned. Bringing in the soldiers, he felt, could only lead to more tension on the reservation.

As far as Charles was concerned, the Ghost Dancers had no intention of starting a conflict with the whites. They were only reacting to the difficult conditions on the reservation. Charles believed that if the government were to take steps to relieve the hunger and poverty on the reservation, the Sioux people would eventually lose interest in the Ghost Dance.

Even though Charles openly expressed his opinions, Daniel Royer, the newly appointed government agent, stuck with his own ideas. Royer, whom the Sioux rightfully called "young-man-afraid-of-his-Indians," had sent a telegram on November

15 requesting the cavalry. He suggested that all the Ghost Dance leaders be arrested and jailed until order on the reservation could be restored.

On the morning of November 20, the soldiers arrived. With their support, the Indian police were asked to carry out Agent Royer's plan. Royer and his supervisor, Agent James McLaughlin, were especially concerned about Sitting Bull and his many supporters. According to the Indian police, Sitting Bull was preparing to move down to the Ghost Dancers' camp. Hearing these reports, Agent McLaughlin, who considered Sitting Bull to be a powerful and dangerous influence, issued a warrant for his arrest.

Just before daybreak on December 15, the Indian police surrounded Sitting Bull's camp at Standing Rock. Several officers entered the old leader's dwelling and quietly placed him under arrest. But somehow word got around the camp that Sitting Bull was in trouble. A crowd of supporters gathered around his home. When the police tried to hustle Sitting Bull away, he cried out for help. Someone shot and wounded Lieutenant Bullhead, one of the Indian policemen. Bullhead turned and shot Sitting Bull dead. A blaze of rifle fire followed. By the time the smoke cleared, Sitting Bull and seven of his supporters, including his seventeen-year-old son Crow Foot, lay dead on his front doorstep. Along with Lieutenant Bullhead, five other policemen had been killed.

News of Sitting Bull's death spread quickly. Throughout the

reservation, many Sioux feared more violence. Expecting the worst, many Pine Ridge residents abandoned their homes and fled the village. In an effort to restore order to the village, Pine Ridge leaders asked Big Foot, another powerful Sioux leader, for his support. They offered him one hundred ponies to come to Pine Ridge. His presence, the Pine Ridge leaders felt, would bring a sense of security to the community.

Government authorities thought otherwise. They became concerned when they heard Big Foot was leading a large number of followers toward Pine Ridge. They believed that he was a strong supporter of the Ghost Dance religion. Was he now coming to seek revenge for Sitting Bull's death?

What the authorities didn't know was that Big Foot had been a Ghost Dance supporter at one time, but in recent months he had lost interest. He had no intention of seeking a conflict. He was only responding to the request made by the Sioux leaders at Pine Ridge.

But as he approached Pine Ridge, government authorities became more concerned and finally the army commander at the agency sent out a party of scouts. Big Foot was told to stay away from Pine Ridge. He agreed and the soldiers left. But on December 23, under pressure from some of his followers, Big Foot started out once again for Pine Ridge. This time Colonel James Forsyth and the Seventh Cavalry were sent out to confront Big Foot and his band.

Government employees at the agency, as well as the Pine

Ridge Sioux, feared the worst. To ease the tension, Elaine Goodale and Charles made arrangements for a Christmas celebration. For a day or two, holiday activities helped to restore a sense of hope and good cheer. And on Christmas Day, Charles and Elaine added to the festivities when they announced their engagement.

But early in the morning of December 29, gunshots were heard in the distance. When the Seventh Cavalry returned at dusk, twenty-five soldiers were dead and another thirty-four wounded. Big Foot's entire band had been wiped out. Later reports indicated that the cavalry had surrounded Big Foot and his supporters near Wounded Knee Creek, and were in the process of taking away their weapons, when one of the Sioux fired a shot. The gunfire that followed left few survivors. One hundred fifty-three Sioux were killed and forty-four wounded. Even women and children were gunned down. As Indian messengers spread the word, tipis surrounding Pine Ridge quickly disappeared, and crowds of Sioux left for the distant canyon country known as the Badlands where they hoped to find refuge.

Meanwhile, a group of army surgeons had set up a field hospital to treat the soldiers. It was up to Charles and several assistants, including Elaine, to provide care for the wounded Sioux. In the mission chapel where the Christmas tree still stood, they set up a temporary clinic—tearing out pews and covering the floor with hay and quilts. The wounded were laid out in rows. Charles and the volunteers stayed up all night caring for them. Despite their best efforts, only a few patients recovered—among them, several children whose parents had been killed.

During the night of December 29, a blizzard swept across the prairie. It wasn't until January 1, 1891, after the storm finally let up, that Charles was able to lead a group of civilians out to look for any remaining survivors of the Wounded Knee incident. About three miles from the site of the massacre, they found the first body. From there on, the dead were scattered everywhere, lying where they had been shot while trying to run away.

When they reached the site of Big Foot's camp, Charles was shocked to find the bodies of so many women and children. Many of the Sioux, some of whom found relatives, started crying aloud and singing death songs. It was all Charles could do to contain his own emotions.

They did find a few survivors. Charles found a small baby wrapped in warm blankets and an old woman, blind and helpless, who was lying under a wagon. Other wounded Sioux who had somehow survived the storm were loaded up in the wagons and taken back to the chapel.

Over the next few days, Charles tried to devote his thoughts to the wounded and how he could best help them. Still, he was haunted by the sights that he had seen at Big Foot's camp. As far as Charles was concerned, Big Foot and his people had never meant to be hostile. They just became frightened when they were forced to surrender their weapons. True, an Indian may have fired the first shot, but why had so many defenseless people been killed? Charles couldn't help but question these actions and again he voiced his thoughts. It was this kind of honesty that soon became his undoing.

Not long after the Wounded Knee tragedy, Charles became embroiled in a conflict with Captain George Leroy Brown, the new agent at Pine Ridge. It all began with a law passed by Congress. The law said that all Sioux Indians not involved in the Wounded Knee conflict would be paid back in cash for any property that had been lost or damaged during the incident. Charles was among those appointed to make sure that the payments were made as intended.

When he heard some of the Sioux people complain that they were not getting their full payments, he wrote to the U.S. Indian commissioner. Hearing of these complaints, Agent Brown was angered that Charles had not come to him first. It was a fair criticism perhaps. On the other hand, Charles didn't know this new agent and he suspected that the agent had intentionally cheated the Indians. Also, he knew he could count on General Morgan, the Indian commissioner, a fair-minded man who had been helpful in providing a hospital and other support for Charles's medical efforts at Pine Ridge.

When General Morgan heard about the situation at Pine Ridge, he sent another agent from the Indian Commission to investigate the case. This agent came out to Pine Ridge, made an investigation, and found that $10,000 had been withheld from the Sioux. The agent reported back to General Morgan, who in turn gave the report to his superior, the secretary of the interior.

But the secretary of the interior refused to accept the report and sent his own agent out to investigate the matter. After a short investigation, this agent reported that there had been no wrongdoing. Charles suspected a cover-up. He requested a leave of absence so that he could go to Washington and present his own case.

Meanwhile, in letters to Commissioner Morgan, Special Agent Brown had criticized Charles, saying that he had left Pine Ridge on several occasions without giving any notice. He also claimed that Charles had been disrespectful. He was especially upset about articles that Elaine had written for Eastern newspapers, attacking the conditions at Pine Ridge.

Charles complained of harassment from Agent Brown. Once, Charles had been called away from the agency to treat a patient. On his way to the patient's camp, he was told by an Indian policeman to return to the agency as fast as possible. Expecting an emergency, Charles hurried back to Pine Ridge—but there wasn't any emergency. Instead, Agent Brown criticized Charles for racing his team of horses.

In September of 1892, Agent Brown sent written requests to the Indian commissioner, asking that Charles be transferred to another agency. In these letters Brown claimed that Charles had done everything possible to weaken his power at the agency. In order for him to get his job done, Brown said, it would be best to have Charles work somewhere else.

Commissioner Morgan offered Charles jobs elsewhere, hoping to solve the conflict with Agent Brown in a way that would suit everybody. But Charles decided to stand his ground. He would not be run out of a job because of an Indian agent who felt threatened.

Then in January of 1893, John Noble, the secretary of the interior, stepped in. All along he had sided with Agent Brown. Now he had decided to take action. He informed General Morgan that unless Charles was willing to accept a position somewhere else, he would have to resign. If Charles refused to resign, he would be suspended. To accept another position, as far as Charles was concerned, was to admit that he had been mistaken in his conflict with Agent Brown. He offered his resignation instead.

It was a harsh blow to Charles, who had shown great dedication in his tireless work for the Sioux at Pine Ridge. Even Secretary Noble had offered nothing but praise for Eastman's abilities as a doctor. At the same time, Noble believed that Agent Brown's authority was more important. The sad ending of his medical service at Pine Ridge was Charles's first lesson in the white world of politics.

Chapter 8

SPREADING THE FAITH

During the difficult times at Pine Ridge, Charles looked to his family for support. When he needed her help and encouragement, Elaine was there for him. They had been married in a New York church on June 18, 1891. Dora Winona, their first child, had been born on May 31, 1892.

Following his resignation from Pine Ridge in the winter of 1893, Charles decided to take his family to St. Paul, Minnesota. Minnesota was, after all, his homeland. It would be good to return to his roots.

After arriving in St. Paul with very little money, Charles immediately began to prepare for the state medical exams; he hoped to set up his own medical practice. Charles passed the grueling three-day test, set up his practice, and then found he was only able to make a modest living—at times barely enough to support his family.

On several occasions, he was told that he could make more money if he advertised himself as offering "Indian medicine." One day, Charles was approached by a St. Paul businessman who expressed interest in backing him financially if he would add "Indian Medicine" to his sign. The man claimed that there were many people interested in alternative cures and healing techniques. Much to the man's surprise, Charles refused. Charles was not a medicine man, nor would he use his heritage to make extra money. He had been trained to use modern medicine.

At times like this, Charles longed to be working with the Indian Service again. He felt a deep disappointment over his experience at Pine Ridge, but he knew he had been fair and honest. Still, he wondered if his resignation had hurt his reputation as a government doctor. Even though he had experienced some success with his own practice by the end of his first year in St. Paul, he was determined to serve his own people again, so he sent out letters inquiring about jobs with the Indian Service.

One day, at about this same time, a stranger came by his office. This man, it turned out, was one of the field secretaries for the Young Men's Christian Association (YMCA)—an organization providing athletic and religious training for young men. He was interested in setting up YMCA programs on western Indian reservations and asked Charles for advice. To Charles, the idea of combining Bible studies with sports and other activities seemed like a good opportunity for young people to develop strength and religious faith. He saw no reason why the YMCA programs wouldn't benefit his people.

His conversation with the man from the YMCA ended with a job offer. The man asked Charles if he would be interested in working as a field director in charge of the YMCA's Indian programs. It was a prospect that appealed to Charles because he would be able to serve his people again. Still, he didn't want to give up the medical profession altogether. He agreed to work for the YMCA if they would agree to educate a young Indian man who would eventually take over the job. Not only would that create an opportunity for someone else, but it would allow Charles to return to his work as a doctor after several years of service with the YMCA. Under these conditions, he started his new job on June 1, 1894.

It was a job that forced Charles to examine his own beliefs. How, for example, could he promote the Christian religion to native people who had often been mistreated by the whites? And how was it that so many Indians who had never been to church seemed so much closer to God than other people, both Indian and white, who went to church all the time?

These were difficult questions for Charles, but they were questions he was willing to grapple with. He believed that there were many similarities between the Christian religion and the native beliefs that he had been taught. For example, Sioux people, like Christians, believed in an afterlife and recognized a supernatural power. He believed that the Great Mystery was the same as the Christian God.

As he traveled throughout the reservations in the western states and up in Canada, Charles gave talks about Jesus, about God, and about physical fitness that were generally well received. He was especially successful with his own Sioux people, partly because he understood their language and their customs. Other tribes were less receptive. One time, after Charles had finished a lecture to a group of Sauk and Fox Indians in Iowa, an older chief stood up and expressed his belief that the whites had little respect for nature or for God. To him, Christianity had little to offer.

There were others, especially some of the tribal elders, who challenged him with their questions and comments, "I have come to the conclusion," said an older man during a Bible study, "that this Jesus was an Indian. He was opposed to material...possessions. He was inclined to peace....These are not the principles upon which the white man has founded his civilization."

Charles couldn't help but agree. There were many times when Christianity and the actions of white people seemed to contradict one another. Greed, as one old warrior pointed out, was a quality that didn't seem to fit with Christian ideals. He compared the Indian way with white civilization: "We owned nothing ... Food was free, land free as sunshine and rain. Who has changed all this? The white man; and yet he says he is a believer in God! He does not seem to inherit any of the traits of his Father, nor does he follow the example set by his brother Christ."

The whites might not follow their own beliefs, but the spirit of Christianity, Charles believed, was the same as the spirit of the old ways. He continued to believe in the YMCA because it offered hope and strength to Indian people who had been forced to give up their traditional life-styles. It was one way he could help his people cope with the poverty and hopelessness Charles so often found on the reservations. He also believed that the Indian people would never be able to return to the old way of life. Their only choice was to take the best of the white world.

So for three years, he continued to travel, helping to set up over forty YMCA's throughout Indian territory. It was during a trip to the Crow reservation in Montana that he happened to meet a missionary from Scotland. During a journey through Manitoba as a young man, the young Scot had met an Indian who talked with great feeling about Jesus and the Bible. This experience had inspired him to become a minister. After returning to Scotland and studying for several years, the young minister returned to America and spent many years telling Indian people about Christianity.

As it turned out, the Indian who had sparked the young man's interest in God and the Bible was none other than Mysterious Medicine, Charles's uncle. Mysterious Medicine also had been converted to Christianity and had changed his name to Joseph Eastman.

On one of his YMCA Canadian trips, Charles traveled to Manitoba and found his uncle living on a farm in a Christian community. After twenty years of separation, it was an emotional reunion for both of them. "When we are old," his uncle said, crying tears of joy, "our hearts are not strong in moments like this. The Great Spirit has been kind to let me see my boy again before I die."

Charles would never forget this man who had helped raise him. Nor would he forget Uncheedah, his beloved grandmother, who had returned to Manitoba to spend her final years. As he stood beside her grave, he savored fond memories of his boyhood in the forests of Canada.

Chapter 9

RETURN OF THE SIOUX DOCTOR

After three years of traveling throughout Indian country, Charles resigned from his position with the YMCA. Not only was he anxious to spend more time with his family (which now included three daughters), he also wanted to bring his medical skills back to the Sioux reservation. Once again, he applied to the Indian Service, and in the meantime, he took a job at Carlisle Indian School in Pennsylvania.

Colonel Richard Henry Pratt, the superintendent at Carlisle, which had been established back in 1879 for the education of Indian students, wanted to promote peaceful relations between Indians and whites. With that goal in mind, he set up an outing program that enabled Indian pupils to live in Christian homes. Charles became the outing agent. It was his responsibility to choose host families and to take care of any difficulties the students had in adapting to their new surroundings.

Charles was also in charge of bringing new students to Carlisle and often traveled out to the reservations to recruit them. Returning from one such trip in December of 1899, Charles caught pneumonia and spent the entire month of January in bed. Elaine was worried. Doctors feared for the worst. But Charles finally recovered and soon he was back on the job.

On September 5, 1900, Charles received a letter offering him the job of government physician at the Crow Creek Agency on the Sioux reservation in South Dakota. He gratefully accepted, anxious to pursue once again what he believed was his true calling. On September 19, Charles and his family arrived in Crow Creek and moved into their new home. It was a small house — fairly cramped quarters for a growing family — but it was a big improvement over Charles's shack at the Pine Ridge Agency.

By October 1, Charles was on the job. Right away, he was faced with great challenges. At that time smallpox epidemics were sweeping through the Indian territories. One of Charles's first tasks was to make sure that the Sioux people at Crow Creek were protected from the disease. He was ordered to disinfect all public buildings at the agency, a big job that required generators and various chemical sprays. Even more of a challenge was the job of vaccinating the Sioux people against smallpox. Charles talked with people all over the reservation to convince them that shots were helpful. Thanks in large part to his efforts, the Sioux at Crow Creek were spared the dreaded disease.

As he always had, Charles made himself available to his patients at all times, and he soon won the respect and trust of the Sioux people at Crow Creek. It seemed, however, that this trust and respect from his patients threatened his relationship with the government agent at Crow Creek.

When Charles first arrived in Crow Creek, he heard rumors and complaints about James H. Stephens, the government agent at that time. According to some of the Sioux, Stephens had been guilty of illegal trading and he also had been neglecting his duties. Charles wanted to avoid any political conflicts and tried to steer clear of any controversy. He was careful not to involve himself in the complaints filed by White Ghost, a local Sioux leader; the Reverend Hachalia Burt, a minister at Crow Creek; and Bishop William Hare, a supporter of Indian rights. All of these men called for the removal of Agent Stephens who was replaced in June of 1901 by Harry Chamberlain. Charles remained quiet—the last thing he needed was another Pine Ridge experience.

Charles was anxious to establish good relations with Chamberlain, who seemed like a well-intentioned man. Charles pledged that he would not become involved in politics at Crow Creek, a promise that he was able to keep—for a while. In July of 1902, Agent Chamberlain accused him of stirring up trouble.

Once again, White Ghost had complained to William Jones, the Indian commissioner, about conditions on the reservation. He had written a letter to Commissioner Jones complaining that Agent Chamberlain had cut off payments and government aid to some Indians—saying that they needed to support themselves. White Ghost also had accused Chamberlain of other misdeeds and had requested permission to come to Washington "with a good interpreter" to discuss these problems further. When Chamberlain heard about this letter to the commission, he assumed right away that Charles was the "good interpreter" and that he had encouraged White Ghost to file a complaint.

Agent Chamberlain then sent his own letter off to the commission, claiming that Charles was the one stirring up trouble. He said Doctor Eastman wanted to visit Washington for his own benefit, and had volunteered his services as the interpreter and encouraged White Ghost to send his letter for that reason. Chamberlain claimed that Charles was guilty of other offenses — offenses that he would ignore if Eastman promised to mind his own business. He then asked the commission to suggest, in a letter, that Charles stick to his medical duties.

A week later, Chamberlain heard about another letter of complaint signed by White Ghost and sent to Alfred Kittredge, a U.S. Senator from South Dakota. He called White Ghost into his office immediately. When White Ghost denied writing the letter, Chamberlain accused Charles of writing it. Reminding Commissioner Jones of similar problems at Pine Ridge, he asked that Charles be transferred to another agency.

He then went on to list a number of reasons why Charles should be removed from his position at Crow Creek. Chamberlain claimed that Charles had been negligent as a physician. Among other things, said Chamberlain, Eastman had left the agency without giving notice and he had refused to treat a blind boy. Charles denied the charges. When he traveled, he always left word with his family about where he went and when he would return. As for the blind boy, Charles had never refused him—or anyone else—treatment. He simply admitted that there was nothing he could do and suggested that perhaps an eye operation by a specialist could help.

Chamberlain argued that Charles lacked the morals and the honesty to continue in his role. The agent claimed that Charles told the Indians that they could perform their dances. Charles argued that he had discouraged dancing, especially on Sundays. Chamberlain told the commissioner that Charles participated in the writing of the complaint letters to Senator Kittredge and to the commissioner. Charles denied it. Then Chamberlain accused Charles of plotting against him. Not true, said Charles.

What was the truth? William Jones, the Indian commissioner, ordered a special investigation at Crow Creek. The investigators were unable to prove that Charles's actions had been immoral in any way. On the other hand, they said that Charles often consulted with White Ghost and other Sioux and that he had met with Thomas Hall, the superintendent of the Indian school at Crow Creek, to discuss poor living conditions on the reservation and Chamberlain's shortcomings as an agent. The investigators also reported that Charles had left the agency on several occasions without informing Agent

Chamberlain, but Charles claimed he had never been told to inform him.

Once again, it seemed as though Charles's ability to develop friendships with the Sioux people had worked against him. Even though he had pledged not to get involved with politics at Crow Creek, he couldn't help but listen to his own people when they approached him with their grievances. The investigators recommended that Charles be sent to work somewhere other than the Sioux reservation. If he was less familiar with the Indian people he was treating, they thought, maybe he wouldn't end up in these difficult situations. But Commissioner Jones had other plans for Charles.

Chapter 10

THE NAME GIVER

On March 5, 1903, Indian Commissioner William Jones offered Charles a new job. Because of the Dawes Act, a law passed by the U.S. Senate in 1887, some members of the Sioux tribe were eligible to receive their own lands on which to homestead. The problem for the government was to determine who was eligible. Because Sioux family members didn't share the same last names, it was hard to tell who belonged to what family. And since family relationships often determined who received land, something had to be done to clear up the situation.

Supporters of the Indian people suggested that the government provide the Sioux and other Indian people with appropriate family names. This would clarify family relationships and make it easier for government officials to decide who was eligible to receive land. Commissioner Jones knew that Charles maintained a good relationship with his people and that he would be better at this job than someone who didn't know the Sioux people or their language. Providing Eastman with a different situation might also help relieve the tensions with Agent Chamberlain at Crow Creek.

Charles decided to take the job and resigned from his position at Crow Creek. He moved his family to White Bear,

Minnesota, a suburb of St. Paul. From there, it wasn't too far to the Sioux reservation in South Dakota where he soon started his fieldwork.

Charles saw his new job as an opportunity to help his people become independent landowners. By making a living at farming or raising livestock, he thought, Indian people would no longer have to depend on the government for survival. And since those who received land allotments also became U.S. citizens, Charles believed that the Dawes Act would help his people to become a part of the white world. Like his father, Charles had come to believe that the only way to survive in the midst of the white world was to become a part of it.

With these thoughts in mind, he began his work at the Sisseton Agency in South Dakota. He soon realized that this job of providing names for the Sioux was a more complex task than he had imagined. Perhaps the greatest challenge was convincing the Sioux people to participate. Charles explained that these new names would enable them to own the land that was rightfully theirs. Gradually, the Sioux people at Sisseton came to trust him.

Generally, what Charles tried to do was select one name — a name that was fairly short and easily pronounced or translated — and then group all the family members under this name. If the father's name was Higheagle, for example, then the wife and children might take "Higheagle" as their last name. They also might be given shorter first names.

Even though Charles believed in the reasons for simplifying the Sioux names, he also tried hard to preserve their meaning and spirit. Names that translated into words like White Bear had a certain beauty, grace, and meaning that he saw no reason to change. Others could be simplified without too much trouble. For example, a woman named "Tateyohnakewastewin," which was hard for whites to say, and which meant "She-Who-Has-A-Beautiful-House," was given the name "Goodhouse." But in some instances, names were hard to translate. In other cases, Charles had a hard time determining which names were considered to be real names and which were just nicknames.

Between 1903 and 1909 Charles revised the names for twenty-five thousand Sioux, who in turn dubbed him the "Name Giver." Even though some beautiful Indian names had to be changed, his work helped clarify family records and made it easier for the government and the Sioux people to establish rights to personal property.

In later years, there would be those who criticized the name-giving project, claiming that it was simply another way for the whites to strip the Sioux of their tradition and culture. The government, they said, was forcing the Indians to accept white names and become just like white people.

What disturbed Charles during his renaming work was the fact that some Indian people were being cheated out of the land that had been allotted to them under the Dawes Act. One of the main reasons for his involvement in the project was to help his people achieve a sense of independence as farmers. When he heard about dishonest whites who were cheating uneducated Indians and gaining title to their lands, he wrote a letter to the Indian commissioner. Commissioner Jones wrote back saying that if Charles was going to make such statements, he would need to have the evidence to back them up. Charles decided that it wasn't his job to be an investigator. Nor was he anxious to stir up any more controversy. For the time being, he decided not to pursue the matter.

One cause that he did pursue during this period was the restoration of treaty payments for the Santee Sioux. In 1837 and 1851, treaties had been signed that guaranteed the Santees a certain amount of money in government aid. Then came the Santee Sioux Uprising in 1862. Responding to poverty and broken government promises, several young Sioux resorted to violence. The battle that followed—the same battle that led to Jacob Eastman's arrest—resulted in the deaths of many innocent people, both Sioux and white. Shortly after the massacres, the government decided to punish the Sioux by putting a halt to treaty payments.

By now, Charles knew something about the way the government worked and he knew people in Washington, D.C. It seemed to him that he could help his people by talking to congressmen and senators and asking them to help restore the old treaty payments. It had been more than thirty years since the uprising. The Santee, he argued, had been punished enough.

In order for the treaty payments to be made again, Congress would have to pass a law and then the Santee Sioux would have to present their case in court. Over a period of twenty years, beginning in the 1890s, Charles pursued the case. He realized that if he were successful his work could bring large financial rewards, not only for the tribe, but also for himself in the form of legal fees.

Over the years, he made numerous trips to Washington, D.C., when he had time away from his other work. Together with his wife Elaine and his brother John, he worked hard to rally congressmen behind the Santee cause. But once again, he became frustrated with the game of politics. Some congressmen asked for money in exchange for their support. Others simply didn't care.

Even at home, Charles had to struggle with politics. He wasn't the only one who wanted to represent the tribe in Washington. James Garvie, a Sioux minister and a former teacher at Santee Normal Training School, felt that he was the best person for the job. Both men had their supporters, and even though Charles finally won out, power struggles within the tribe often made his job more difficult.

Years later, after Congress passed a law enabling the Sioux to go to court, other lawyers were appointed to represent the tribe. When the Santee finally won their case in the U.S. Court of Claims, Charles received only a small portion of the payment—much less than he thought he deserved for all the work he had done on the case over the years. Some Santees, Garvie among them, criticized him when he asked for more money, and to some extent maybe they were right. Maybe Charles had been expecting too much of a reward for his own efforts.

Still, he could take some of the credit. His time, his persistence, and his willingness to confront the often unpleasant world of politics also showed his dedication to the Santee people.

Chapter 11

BACK TO THE WOODS

As a doctor, as a fieldworker for the YMCA, and as the Sioux "Name Giver," Charles had spent much of his life bringing the whites' ways to the Indian people. But there were also aspects of his Indian background from which Charles believed the whites could learn. Of all the native beliefs and traditions that he had been exposed to as a boy, perhaps none was more important than the deep respect and love for nature that Charles learned from his grandmother and uncle.

Throughout his life, Charles always had been able to find peace and strength in the wilderness, so it was with great pleasure that he accepted a job in the lake country of northern Minnesota and southern Ontario in the summer of 1910. He had been asked by the University of Pennsylvania to collect Indian artifacts from the Ojibway people who lived in this region.

As he canoed farther into Ojibway territory, he felt like he was traveling back in time. Drifting past the pine-covered islands and thick swampy forests, he saw fewer signs of whites. In fact, it seemed that the Ojibway, more than any other tribe he knew of, had avoided whites. They still lived the old way—hunting, fishing, and gathering wild rice and berries.

During his boyhood, the Ojibway and the Sioux often had

been enemies. As a Sioux, Charles wondered how well he would be received in their camps now. At his first stop, he was welcomed by Majigabo, the chief of the Leech Lake Ojibway. The chief invited Charles to attend an Ojibway dance where Charles listened to the steady beat of the moosehide drum in a thatch-roofed hall. This was a ceremony that probably had not changed much since the days of his boyhood.

Majigabo told Charles about a battle with whites. Several years earlier, white soldiers had come to subdue the Ojibway, but his islanders fought back and the whites had not returned. "They can take everything else," Majigabo said, "but they must leave me and these island people alone." Charles respected the chief and his determination to hold onto the old ways. He was glad that there were still places where Indian people practiced the old ways.

As he continued on his journey, Charles met a band of Ojibway hunters at Red Lake. They were just returning from a successful moose hunt. At first, they were suspicious of this Sioux stranger. As they continued to talk, some of them even recalled battles with Charles's relatives. But Charles demonstrated his goodwill along with his knowledge and respect for their customs, and gradually they accepted him.

As a collector for the museum, Charles was supposed to gather samples of Ojibway artwork, especially those items that were older and used in ceremonies. To do that, he had to make friends with the Ojibway people he met at Red Lake and elsewhere. After feasting and trading presents with tribal leaders, he often was shown objects of historical or religious interest that whites never would have been allowed to see. Occasionally, he was presented with artifacts of great value, which he later turned over to the museum.

Accompanied by an Ojibway guide, Charles journeyed farther into the wilderness. By now it was the middle of August—time for the wild rice harvest. They passed Ojibway families shaking the kernels of wild rice stalks into their canoes. When the canoes were half full they were emptied along the shore. Then the harvesters would return to the watery fields for more.

In the early mornings, Charles and his guide passed Ojibway people pulling nets full of fish out of the water. One day, Charles caught a sturgeon that weighed 150 pounds. Deer and moose also were plentiful. On one of the islands they passed, Charles counted eight moose in one place.

Near an area known as Seine Bay, Charles witnessed a loon hunt. The loon, a ducklike bird whose eerie call echoed through the lake country, had a fishy flavor the Ojibway seemed to like. When approached, a loon would dive underwater. Hunters followed in their canoes trying to guess where the bird would come back up. Sometimes they would pop up as much as a quarter of a mile away. After several dives, the birds usually got tired and were easily caught.

The more Charles saw of the Ojibway's territory and the more he witnessed their traditional ways, the more he thought of his own boyhood. Once again, he was becoming very comfortable in the North Woods. It became harder and harder to think about leaving, but as the summer came to an end and the nights began to get cooler, he knew it was time.

One day on the journey homeward, Charles and his guide stopped at an abandoned Indian village. There in a clearing stood rows of tidy homes, each one carefully made with the bark of the trees that grew on the island. Inside these homes were dishes, clothing, and piles of furs. Whoever lived here had left in a hurry. Intrigued by this empty village, Charles continued to look around, and decided that they should spend the night.

Later on, as they sat around a fire in one of the cabins, the guide told Charles that a band of Indians had stayed in this village every winter for many years. One winter, some of their children caught a strange sickness. After several had died, the rest of the villagers fled in fear, leaving all their belongings behind.

As the fire died down and the night grew still, Charles couldn't help but feel the mystery of this place. Then he heard the scratching. Something was scratching on the cabin door. Charles and his guide looked at one another across the fire. Then they heard the noise again. Charles got out his gun and walked over to the door. He opened the door, took a step back, and there, standing up on its hind legs, was the biggest turtle he had ever seen. It must have come by to see who the intruders were, Charles thought. Then the turtle waddled off into the darkness.

At the end leg of his journey, Charles boarded a gasoline-powered passenger boat that was to take him out to the town of International Falls. Wildfires had been raging through the forest that surrounded the lake and the air was filled with smoke, making it hard for the pilot to steer his boat. As it got dark, the boat motored into a narrow channel between several islands. Then the wind began to blow.

Fearing that they would be blown off course, the pilot decided to try to find a harbor on one of the islands. As he turned the boat in toward the island, a huge wave caught the boat broadside, smashed through windows, and put out all the lights. Without lights, there was no way to navigate the boat through the rocky island channels; so Charles, the pilot, and two other passengers decided to jump and swim for it. The boat and all its freight disappeared into the rainy night. Somehow the crew was able to swim ashore. Charles hoped he would find some kind of wild game, but this island was too small. When a rescue boat finally arrived several days later, it was a happy occasion.

For Charles, the journey into Ojibway territory had not only been an adventure, it also had enabled him to experience the wilderness life again. It reminded him of the value of an outdoor life, and it inspired him to get involved with an educational organization that was just getting started.

As cities and towns had grown bigger and bigger, and the American frontier had all but disappeared, there were those who believed that young people should have the opportunity to experience nature and the wilderness. With this idea in mind, William D. Boyce, Ernest Thompson Seton, and Daniel Carter Beard founded the Boy Scouts of America. In 1910, Charles offered his assistance to the new organization.

Charles believed in the Boy Scout cause. It pleased him that Scouts and Campfire Girls alike were being taught to appreciate the old Indian ways. And as far as Seton was concerned, Charles was the perfect teacher and role model. Not only did he know how to live in the woods, he knew how to tell a good story. As a guest speaker and later as a camp director, he entertained scout troops with the tales he had been told as a boy, many of which he included later in his popular books.

His experiences with the Boy Scouts and Campfire Girls inspired Charles to start his own summer camp. "The School of the Woods," as the Eastmans called their camp, was originally set up for girls only. In July of 1915, the first group of campers came to stay with the Eastmans on the shores of a New Hampshire lake. Elaine helped run the camp as did the three oldest Eastman daughters—Dora, Irene, and Virginia— who worked as counselors. Even the younger children— Ohiyesa II, Eleanor, and Florence—helped out with other camp activities.

After their first successful season, the Eastmans made their camp even bigger and opened it to boys too. Eager campers filled the tents and cabins along the lakeshore for the next few years, providing a steady income for the Eastmans. But as far as Charles was concerned, the camp was more than a business. It was a way to spread the love of nature that he had been taught as a child.

The YMCA building at White Clay, Pine Ridge Reservation in South Dakota

Chapter 12

The Indian Cause

As a young man living along the edge of two very different worlds, Charles had tried to combine the best aspects of his native upbringing with those of the white world. As a doctor, he took his knowledge of medicine to the Sioux people. During his job with the YMCA, he shared his Christian faith with the Indian nations. These were some of the elements of white America that were good—elements, he felt, that could only help his people.

His work with the Boy Scouts was one way Charles found to introduce the Indian's appreciation of nature and the great outdoors to white America. His School of the Woods was another. But his abilities as a storyteller and lecturer were perhaps his most effective tools in educating white America about the Indian.

Surrounded by his homeland after moving back to St. Paul in 1893, Charles felt a strong urge to share the adventures of his boyhood. At first, he simply wrote down his memories for the benefit of his own children. When Elaine read what he had written, she suggested he send his stories to a young people's magazine called *St. Nicholas*. Thanks in part to Elaine's ability to edit what Charles wrote, the stories were accepted. Later, she helped Charles combine these stories into *Indian*

Boyhood, his first book, which was published in 1902.

It was Charles's intention to present an accurate picture of the Indian people and their way of life. Too often white people looked upon the Indian people as ignorant and backward. In his writing and lecturing, Charles was quick to correct them, pointing out the many strengths and contributions of America's native people. In addition to their deep respect for nature, Charles wrote about the beauty of their arts and crafts. Indian people, he said, also had developed their own herbal medicines and farming techniques. They knew, as well as anyone, how to live off the land.

As he became recognized for his writing, Charles was often invited to lecture about his life and about Indian people. Often he would deliver his speeches wearing an eagle-feathered warbonnet and beaded buckskin clothes. Sometimes he carried a tomahawk pipe. This was a tomahawk with a hollow shaft or stem and a pipe bowl set across from the blade of the hatchet at one end.

A strikingly handsome man, Charles had a powerful voice, a strong stage presence, and was much in demand as a speaker. He believed that if he could help white America see the world from an Indian point of view, he could break down their prejudices.

And if he could do that, maybe relations between the two cultures would improve. In his writings and lectures, Charles never hesitated to criticize whites for their attitudes toward

Indian people. For example, he openly challenged the prejudices of many white missionaries who tried to convert Indian people to Christianity. To Charles, Indian beliefs and those of Christianity had a lot in common, but the missionaries thought otherwise. They held that only their own beliefs and stories were true.

To make his point, Charles had a favorite story. A missionary on one of the reservations told a group of Indians about Adam and Eve. When the Indians told the missionary an Indian creation story, he angrily denounced it as false. The Indians were perplexed: they believed his story, why didn't he believe theirs? As far as Charles was concerned, there were truths in both the Indian and white religions. Neither one was right or wrong.

Charles also criticized the government for poor treatment of the Indian people. One of his most common criticisms focused on the reservations themselves. Drawing from his own experiences, he pointed out that many of the reservations were located on dry lands where farming was difficult, if not impossible. Many Indian people who had once been self-sufficient were now dependent on the government for food handouts.

Charles also lashed out at the Indian Service. A government agency set up to serve the Indian people should be run by educated Indians, he said. Charles admitted that there were some good people in the Indian Service but that they were outnumbered. Too often, the Indian agencies were run by whites who were more interested in their own reputations and power than they were in the people they were supposed to be serving.

But Charles wasn't satisfied just to sit back and criticize. As early as 1899, he expressed interest in setting up an Indian organization to help Indian people. In April of 1911, he was invited, along with five other prominent Indian people, to a meeting at Ohio State University to explore the possibilities for such an organization. Some of the other Indian participants were Thomas L. Sloan, a lawyer from the Omaha tribe; Charles E. Daganett, a Peoria Indian who worked for the government; Laura M. Cornelius, from the Oneida tribe in Wisconsin; Carlos Montezuma, a doctor from the Yavapai tribe; and Henry Standing Bear, a Sioux from Pine Ridge. The idea was to include members of all the different tribes in an association that would stand up for the interests of the Indian people.

This first meeting of the Society for American Indians, SAI as it later came to be called, was not without its disagreements. Some members of the group felt that the organization should work closely with the government to improve the quality of life for Indian people. Others, like Charles, who had less confidence in the Indian Service, believed that the society should focus more on providing its own social programs for Indian people instead of leaving it to the government. When a majority voted to try to *assist* the Indian Service, Charles became less enthusiastic about the SAI. Nevertheless, he continued to support the organization and was elected president of the SAI in 1918.

As president of the SAI, Charles campaigned for a cause that he strongly believed in. He wanted to see to it that all Indian people were made United States citizens. After all, there were as many as ten thousand Indians, one of whom was his son, who fought for the United States in World War I. Shouldn't they enjoy the same privileges of citizenship as all the white soldiers who fought in the war? Charles was dedicated to this cause and was working hard to achieve his goals when tragedy struck. A flu epidemic left Elaine and three of his daughters very sick. On October 23, 1918, Irene, his second daughter, died.

After gathering with his family for Irene's funeral Charles returned, deeply saddened, to his duties as president of the SAI. He continued to fight for the rights of his people, but family problems continued to plague him. Money was part of the trouble. The summer camp was no longer as busy as it once had been and book royalties were decreasing. Charles barely had enough to support his family. Tensions were mounting with Elaine.

They had always had their differences, especially when it came to the education of the Indian people. Unlike Charles, Elaine believed that Indians should accept the white way of life altogether and reject all the old Indian traditions—only in that way would they be able to function in society. She was especially critical of the grandmother's role in the Indian family. It was the grandmother, she said, who often expressed dislike for whites. And it was the grandmother who held onto the old ways. Charles always had respected his own grandmother. He also believed that many of the old ways were valuable and worth preserving. Disagreements over these issues may have been a source of the tension between Charles and Elaine.

Elaine had been a strong force in Charles's life. She was the one who got Charles started on his writing career. She made all the arrangements when he went on his lecture tours. And she was responsible for editing and rewriting all of his books. Perhaps Charles felt as though she had too much control over him. Maybe he resented her dominance when it came to his writing.

There also had been periods of their life when Charles had been away from home for great lengths of time, as for example, when he was working for the YMCA. With all that separation, had they just grown apart? Was it true, as some people suggested, that Charles had expressed interest in other women? Did Elaine decide they were simply too far apart in their beliefs and attitudes?

No one really knows. But in August of 1921, Charles and Elaine separated after thirty years of marriage—a sign, perhaps, that it was getting harder and harder for Charles to live up to other people's expectations.

Chapter 13

THE END OF THE TRAIL

Between the years of 1911 and 1918, Charles Eastman published six books, many of them best-sellers translated into several different languages. Those sympathetic to the Indian cause pointed to his accomplishments as proof that an Indian with a good education could succeed in white society. Charles Eastman had become America's most famous Indian.

Because of the pressure Charles felt to succeed, disappointments were harder to take. Along with his successes, there were, after all, plenty of struggles—many of them had to do with money. Even though his books became increasingly popular, he was rarely able to support a big family on the royalties from them. His summer camp had been successful for several years, but eventually he had to depend on other skills to make a living. Lecturing offered some security, but it also meant time away from home.

In April of 1923, he decided to take a job with the Indian Service partly because he needed the money. The Indian Service, after all, was the same government agency that he often had blamed for the poor living conditions on the reservations. Perhaps he felt that he could improve the system and earn some badly needed income at the same time.

Whatever the case, he took the job of Indian inspector, which involved, once again, a great deal of traveling out to the reservations. If there was a conflict between the agency and the people on the reservation, it was up to Charles to investigate the matter. For a man in his mid-sixties, it was a demanding job. At times the paperwork alone overwhelmed him. Even more draining was his involvement in the usual political conflicts. As a younger man at Pine Ridge and later at Crow Creek, he had been able to fight the battles. Now they wore him out. By the spring of 1925, his health was failing. On March 20, he resigned.

But soon he was active again. After taking some time to regain his strength, Charles turned once again to the lecture halls for his livelihood. After one of his speaking engagements, a wealthy New York woman asked him if he would be willing to go on a two-month lecture tour in England. Charles gratefully accepted. He gave speeches at English schools and universities and even went on a fox hunt with a group of British lords.

Upon his return to the United States, he found that he was as well known as ever, despite the fact that he had not published a book for a number of years. He had been writing, but it was much harder to complete a project now, especially since he no longer had Elaine's assistance.

That didn't hurt his reputation, however. He was recognized as a spokesman for his people, and much to his delight, many of his ideas seemed to be finding favor with more and more people. As Charles entered his seventies, it seemed as though white people were becoming more receptive to suggestions for improving health care and providing better educational opportunities on the reservations.

Still, there was much work to be done. At times his son, Ohiyesa II, tried to convince him to rest, but Charles rarely slowed down. He continued to travel and speak out on behalf of his people, and he was often honored for his efforts. His old classmates at Dartmouth expressed their admiration for him at class reunions. He was one of a selected group invited to Mark Twain's seventieth birthday party. And at the Chicago World's Fair in 1933, the Indian Council Fire, an organization representing many different tribes, presented him with an award for "the most distinguished achievements by an American Indian."

In January of 1939, Charles suffered a heart attack. Doctors at a hospital in Detroit, Michigan, examined him on January 7 and decided there was nothing they could do. On January 8, at the age of eighty, Charles Eastman died.

In retrospect, Charles was among a unique group of American Indians in the late nineteenth and early twentieth century who were familiar with life in two very different cultures. Charles was comfortable wearing a tie and a starched collar but he also felt at ease delivering his lectures in a Sioux warbonnet. At times, he may have become disillusioned with the white world, especially when it came to politics, but he refused to turn his back on those qualities of white culture that he thought were worthwhile.

There had always been those people who wanted to see the Indian people give themselves entirely over to the whites' culture. Even his wife Elaine believed that Indian culture was better left behind in the deep woods. Still, Charles never abandoned his roots.

In his own way, he returned to them during his final years, spending the warmer months at an isolated cabin on an island in Lake Huron. This he built himself when he was well into his sixties. It was too late to return to the old ways he had known as a boy, the whites had changed all that; but Charles could still watch the deer and moose. He could still listen to the birds sing. He could still walk the trails through trees so thick they covered the sky. And in the deep silence, he could still feel the presence of the Great Mystery. Here he knew he was always at home.

Charles Eastman 1858-1939

1858 Oyihesa (Charles Alexander Eastman) is born on a Santee Sioux Reservation near Redwood Falls, Minnesota. Mary Nancy Eastman, Charles's mother, dies. Minnesota becomes a U.S. state. An "Expedition Against Northern Indians" is carried out by U.S. army troops to discourage attacks on Washington state settlements. First Atlantic cable is completed by Cyrus W. Field, but it fails to operate. The Lincoln-Douglas debates are held in Illinois. The Suez Canal Company is formed to build a canal in Egypt linking the Mediterranean and Red seas. The National Association of Baseball Players is organized in America.

1859 Oregon becomes a U.S. state. First commercially productive oil well is drilled near Titusville, Pennsylvania. Charles Darwin writes *On the Origin of Species*. The steamroller is invented. Work on the Suez Canal is begun under the direction of Ferdinand de Lesseps.

1860 Abraham Lincoln is elected president. The first pony-express line is started between Sacramento, California, and St. Joseph, Missouri. The first horse-drawn tram begins operation.

1861 Kansas becomes a U.S. state. American Civil War begins (ends 1865). Seven Southern states set up the Confederate States of America with Jefferson Davis as president. Confederate forces repel Union forces at the Battle of Bull Run. First transcontinental telegraph line is put in operation.

1862 The Santee Sioux in Minnesota rebel against mistreatment by white people on their reservation and kill about 800 settlers; as punishment, their land is confiscated and the Sioux are moved to Dakota Territory. Land Grant Act is approved, eventually leading to the establishment of the state university system. Swiss philanthropist Jean Henri Dunant proposes the foundation of an international relief organization—the Red Cross. Many Civil War veterans settle in Western states under free land terms of the 1862 Homestead Act.

1863 West Virginia becomes a U.S. state. Arizona and Idaho are organized as Indian Territories. Confederates lose Battle of Gettysburg. Whitestone Indian battle in North Dakota. Colonel Kit Carson is ordered to subdue Navajo Indians in New Mexico. Gold is discovered on Nez Perce Reservation; U.S. commissioners fraudulently reduce the reservation size. Lincoln issues the Emancipation Proclamation, freeing "all slaves in areas still in rebellion." Congress establishes free mail delivery. Roller skating is introduced to America.

1864 Nevada becomes a U.S. state. During the Sand Creek massacre of Cheyenne and Arapaho Indians in Colorado, some 900 U.S. cavalrymen kill 150 to 500 Indian men, women, and children (the tribes were under an American flag when attacked by U.S. army). Union General William T. Sherman marches through Georgia to the sea. Abraham Lincoln is reelected president. "In God We Trust" first appears on U.S. coins.

1865 Confederate General Robert E. Lee surrenders at Appomattox Court House, Virginia; General Ely Parker, a Seneca, drafts terms of surrender; the American Civil War ends. President Lincoln is assassinated; he is succeeded by Vice-president Andrew Johnson. The Thirteenth Amendment, abolishing slavery, takes effect. Red Cloud, an Oglala Indian chief, leads Sioux warriors to halt the construction of the Powder River Road in Montana. The first sleeping cars, designed by George Pullman, appear in the U.S.

1866 The Fourteenth Amendment, which states that no person can be deprived "of life, liberty, or property without due process of law" is passed. A U.S. army detachment of more than 80 is ambushed and totally wiped out by the Indians under Chief High Backbone in northern Wyoming. Ku Klux Klan is formed secretly in the South. Alfred Nobel invents dynamite. Edward Degas begins to paint ballet scenes. Jacob Eastman (Many Lightnings), Charles's father, is released from prison (in since 1862). Western half of the Indian Territory (Oklahoma) is ceded to the U.S.

1867 Nebraska becomes a U.S. state. Alaska is sold to the U.S. by Russia for $7.2 million. The British North America Act establishes the Dominion of Canada. Gold is discovered in Wyoming. By the Treaty of Medicine Lodge, the southern Cheyenne Indians are assigned a reservation in Oklahoma. Diamonds are discovered in South Africa. David Livingston explores the Congo. The Paris World's Fair introduces Japanese art to the West.

1868 Second Treaty of Port Laramie grants Sioux Indians exclusive possession of the area in South Dakota west of the Missouri River. Alabama, Arkansas, Florida, Louisiana, North Carolina, and South Carolina are readmitted to the Union after the Civil War. The game of badminton is devised in England.

1869 General Ulysses S. Grant is inaugurated as U.S. president. Women suffrage law (the right to vote) passes in the Territory of Wyoming. First population census is taken in Argentina. Suez Canal is opened. Mahatma Gandhi, Indian nationalist leader, is born (died 1948). Jacob Eastman and several other Santee Sioux families establish the community of Flandreau, Minnesota.

1870 Women are admitted to the University of Michigan, Ann Arbor, for the first time since its founding in 1817. Congress appropriates funds for federally administered education in Indian schools.

1871 Congress ends further Indian treaties, and Indians are thereafter governed by congressional legislation agreements and executive agreements. Great Fire destroys Chicago. Trade unions are legalized in Britain.

1872 First U.S. national park, Yellowstone in Wyoming, is established.

1873 The Modoc War (1872-73), between the U.S. army and Modoc Indians about their refusal to settle on Klamath Reservation in Oregon, ends with the hanging of tribal leaders. Charles Eastman, with his father, returns from Canada to Flandreau, Minnesota; he joins the Mission School. Major General George Crook successfully drives most Arizona Apache Indians onto reservations. First U.S. postal card is issued. First railroad reaches North Dakota, bringing many homesteaders.

1874 Gold is discovered on the Sioux Reservation; miners rush in. Adobe Walls Comanche and the army battle in northern Texas. The first American zoo is established in Philadelphia. Charles joins the Santee Normal School in Santee, Nebraska, where John Eastman, Charles's brother, is a teacher (John later becomes a prominent Presbyterian minister).

1875 England purchases Suez Canal shares. Rebellion against Spain begins in Cuba. A civil rights act gives blacks equal rights in public places, though school integration is not included; Supreme Court declares the act invalid in 1883. Seth Eastman, Charles's grandfather and an artist, dies.

1876 Colorado becomes a U.S. state. Ponca Indians are moved from Dakota Territory to the Indian Territory in Oklahoma, where a third of the tribe perishes under harsh climate and scarcity of food. The Sioux Indian uprisings reach their peak when Dakota and Cheyenne destroy General George Custer's troops at Little Bighorn in Montana. Secretary of War William Belknap is impeached for taking bribes for the sale of trading posts in Indian Territory. The Indian Act is passed by the Dominion Parliament in Canada, recognizing the government's responsibility for health, education, and welfare of Indians. Alexander Graham Bell patents the telephone. Mark Twain publishes *The Adventures of Tom Sawyer.* Jacob Eastman dies. Charles enrolls in Beloit College in Wisconsin.

1877 The U.S. government gives Sioux Indians all Ponca lands in Dakota and Nebraska. Refusal of Nez Perce Indians to live on an Idaho reservation leads to the Nez Perce War — 239 Indians die and 266 persons from the U.S. die. Rutherford B. Hayes is declared the winner of 1876 presidential elections. Reconstruction of the South ends. After discovery of gold on their land, the Sioux Indians are forced to relinquish their land, and the "Great Dakota Boom" begins (1879). Indian chief Crazy Horse is murdered following his surrender.

1878 Congress appropriates the first funds for Indian police forces. Thomas Edison invents the incandescent electric lamp.

1879 Ponca leader, Chief Standing Bear, and a group of his people return to Dakota without permission; they are arrested and put into prison. In a landmark decision, *United States ex. rel. Standing Bear vs. Crook,* Ponca chief Standing Bear and his loyal friends are freed from prison. A large number of Indians are killed in an attempt by Chief Dull Knife and his band to escape an Oklahoma reservation and return to their northern homeland. Charles joins Knox College in Tennessee. Carlisle Indian School is established in Pennsylvania. Construction of the Panama Canal to connect the Atlantic and Pacific oceans begins.

1880 A bill is passed in Congress restoring land at Niobrora (Nebraska) to Poncas. James Garfield is elected president. France annexes the island of Tahiti. Department of Indian Affairs is established in Canada.

1881 President Garfield is assassinated; Vice-president Chester A. Arthur becomes president. Helen Hunt Jackson's *A Century of Dishonor* about mistreatment of Indians is published. Indian Shaker church is registered in the state of Washington. Sioux and Cheyenne resistance ends with the surrender of Sioux chief Sitting Bull, returning from Canada.

1882 New York City installs first electric street lamps. U.S. bans Chinese immigration for the next ten years. A world exhibition opens in Moscow, Russia. American Baseball Association is founded.

1883 World's first skyscraper, ten stories high, is built in Chicago. New York's Brooklyn Bridge opens. The Oriental Express — from Paris, France, to Istanbul, Turkey — makes its first run. Charles enrolls at Dartmouth College in Hanover, New Hampshire.

1884 France presents the Statue of Liberty to the U.S. Grover Cleveland is elected president. Indian police force is established on 48 of the 60 agencies (reservations).

1885 Almost unlimited power of the Indian police is curtailed by the Major Crimes Act of Congress. Civil War Union General Ulysses S. Grant dies. Louis Pasteur develops a rabies vaccine.

1886 Geronimo, the Apache resistance Indian leader, surrenders, thus ending the long and bloody Apache Wars of New Mexico and Arizona. Federation of Labor is founded. Canadian Pacific Railway is completed. Slavery is abolished in Cuba.

1887 The Dawes Severalty Act (General Allotment Act) is passed by Congress (later amended in 1891, 1906, and 1910); the act challenges the whole Indian reservation system; it grants citizenship to those Omahas who took land allotments. Area under tribal landholdings totals 138 million acres (reduced to 47 million acres by 1934). The first regulatory commission of the U.S., the Interstate Commerce Commission, is established. Charles graduates with honors from Dartmouth College with a B.S. degree.

1888 Benjamin Harrison is elected president. Sioux Indians suffer great loss as herds of their cattle are killed by diseases and the severe winter.

1889 South Dakota, North Dakota, Montana, and Washington become U.S. states. Oklahoma is opened to non-Indian white settlement. United States Congress passes a law dividing the Sioux Territory into six smaller reservations. The first run for homesteading, by non-Indian settlers, takes place in Oklahoma. Epidemics sweep through the Pine Ridge Reservation. Barnum and Bailey's circus opens in London.

1890 A last major conflict between Indians and U.S. troops, the massacre at Wounded Knee, takes place in South Dakota; 153 Sioux are killed and 44 wounded. Daughters of the American Revolution (DAR) is founded in Washington, D.C. Japan holds its first general elections. Influenza epidemics flare up around the world. Charles graduates with a medical degree from Boston University — one of the first M.D. degrees granted to an Indian student; he joins the Pine Ridge Agency as a government doctor for the Indian Health Service. The Ghost Dance religion begins to take a strong hold among the Sioux Indians.

1891 Charles marries poet, educator, social worker Elaine Goodale. Earthquake in Japan kills 10,000 people. Famine sweeps Russia. Trans-Siberian railroad construction begins.

1892 Grover Cleveland is elected president. Agent George Leroy Brown sends a written request to the Indian commissioner to transfer Charles to another agency. Dora Winona, Charles's and Elaine's first daughter, is born.

1893 The World's Columbian Exposition opens in Chicago. Henry Ford constructs his first automobile. France acquires protectorate over Laos. Charles resigns from his position as government doctor at the Pine Ridge Reservation and moves to St. Paul, Minnesota.

1894 Charles joins YMCA as a field director and starts establishing Indian YMCA groups (some 40 between 1894-97). Korea and Japan declare war on China. Hawaii becomes a republic, following a *coup d'etat.* Uganda becomes a British protectorate.

1895 Chinese are defeated in war with Japan. Cuba begins fighting Spain for independence. King C. Gillette invents the safety razor. Armenians are massacred in Turkey.

1896 Utah becomes a U.S. state. William McKinley is elected president. Mary Church Terrell helps found the National Association of Colored Women. Klondike Gold Rush begins in Alaska.

1897 Charles starts working as a lobbyist in Washington, D.C. for the Santee Sioux (finishes in 1899). William McKinley is inaugurated as U.S. president. First U.S. subway line opens in Boston, Massachusetts. Severe famine hits India. Slavery is abolished in Zanzibar.

1898 U.S. annexes independent republic of Hawaii. Spanish-American War begins, and ends in Treaty of Paris. U.S. acquires the Philippines, Puerto Rico, and Guam. Cuba gains independence from Spain.

1899 Charles becomes the outing agent for the Carlisle Indian School in Pennsylvania. There are about 225 day schools and 148 federally managed boarding schools for Indians, attended by some 20,000 Indian children.

1900 Charles is appointed as an Indian agency physician at the Crow Creek Reservation in South Dakota. William McKinley is reelected president. Bubonic plague epidemic breaks out in the U.S. Australian Commonwealth is proclaimed. Carry Nation, a Kansas prohibitionist, begins raiding saloons with a hatchet.

1901 President William McKinley is assassinated; Theodore Roosevelt becomes president. First Nobel prizes are awarded from a fund left by Alfred Nobel, inventor of dynamite.

1902 Charles is accused of stirring up trouble at the Crow Creek Reservation; he writes *Indian Boyhood*. Cuba becomes an independent republic. Aswan Dam opens in Egypt. U.S. acquires perpetual control over Panama Canal.

1903 President Theodore Roosevelt appoints Charles to revise Sioux allotments so that all Indians receive a fair share of the funds and can protect their title to land (result of Dawes Act). Charles is dubbed "Name Giver" as he gives short, precise names to some 25,000 Sioux Indians. Orville and Wilbur Wright fly the first airplane at Kitty Hawk, North Carolina. White settlement of Alaskan frontier begins.

1904 Theodore Roosevelt is elected to a second presidential term. Russia declares war on Japan. Deaf and blind Helen Keller is graduated from Radcliffe College.

1905 Russo-Japanese War ends in Treaty of Portsmouth.

1906 First radio broadcast of a voice and music program takes place. Zuider Zee drainage scheme to reclaim farmland begins in The Netherlands. San Francisco earthquake kills 700 people and $400 million property is lost.

1907 Oklahoma becomes a U.S. state. President Roosevelt bars Japanese immigration. First electric washing machine is invented in Chicago. Second Sunday in May is established as Mother's Day in Philadelphia.

1908 William Howard Taft is elected president. Ford Motor Company manufactures the first Model T car. Earthquake in southern Calabria and Sicily (in Italy) kills 150,000. Wilbur Wright flies 30 miles in 40 minutes. Simone de Beauvoir, French feminist author, is born.

1909 National Association for the Advancement of Colored People (NAACP) is founded. Explorer Robert E. Peary reaches the North Pole.

1910 Charles is asked by the University of Pennsylvania to collect Indian artifacts from the Ojibway Indians. Charles helps to establish the Boy Scouts of America. National Urban League is formed to help blacks adjust economically and socially to city life. China abolishes slavery. Florence Nightingale dies (born 1820). Japan annexes Korea. Father's Day is celebrated for the first time in Spokane, Washington.

1911 Charles writes *The Soul of the Indian*. Charles is invited to Ohio State University to set up an Indian organization. Chinese revolution begins; Manchu Dynasty falls; Chinese Republic is proclaimed, with Sun Yat-sen as president. Explorer Roald Amundsen reaches the South Pole.

1912 Woodrow Wilson is elected president. The *Titanic* hits an iceberg and sinks on its maiden voyage, drowning 1,513 people.

1913 Balkan Wars begin. Mahatma Gandhi is arrested in India for leading passive resistance movement. Chiricahua Apache Indians are allowed either to take land allotments in Oklahoma or to live in New Mexico on the Mescalero Reservation.

1914 World War I begins. Panama Canal opens.

1915 Albert Einstein introduces his general theory of relativity. Alexander Graham Bell and Thomas Watson hold the first transcontinental telephone conversation.

The Eastmans establish their own summer camp "The School of the Woods" in New Hampshire.

1916 Charles writes *From the Deep Woods to Civilization.* Woodrow Wilson is reelected president.

1917 U.S. declares war on Germany and enters World War I. Bolshevik revolution begins in St. Petersburg, Russia. First jazz phonograph recordings are made.

1918 Charles is elected president of the Society for American Indians (SAI); his second daughter, Irene, dies from influenza. World War I ends. Austria, Hungary, Bavaria, and Germany become republics. Airmail service and daylight saving time begin in U.S.

1919 Eighteenth Amendment passes, prohibiting the sale of alcoholic beverages. First League of Nations meeting is held in Paris, France.

1920 Warren G. Harding is elected president. Nineteenth Amendment gives women the right to vote.

1921 Charles and Elaine are separated after 30 years of marriage. U.S. signs postwar treaties with Germany, Austria, and Hungary. Paris Conference of Allies sets German war debts at $33 million.

1922 Union of Soviet Socialist Republics (U.S.S.R.) is formed. Benito Mussolini gains dictatorial power in Italy. The first All-Pueblo Indian Council meeting is held.

1923 Charles accepts a job as an Indian inspector (1923-25) with the Indian Service; he also becomes a member (til 1925) of the Committee of One Hundred (a reform panel). President Warren G. Harding dies; Calvin Coolidge becomes president.

1924 Calvin Coolidge wins presidential election. J. Edgar Hoover becomes head of what is to become the Federal Bureau of Investigation (FBI). Congress authorizes the Meriam Survey of conditions on Indian reservations. All Indians are made full citizens by an act of Congress.

1925 As Indian inspector Charles is appointed to verify the final resting place of Sacagawea—the guide to Lewis and Clark Expedition—on the Wind River Reservation in Wyoming. Reza Khan becomes shah of Iran and establishes the Pahlavi Dynasty.

1926 Robert H. Goddard develops the first liquid-fuel rocket.

1927 Charles A. Lindbergh makes first solo airplane flight across the Atlantic. Joseph Stalin takes power in the U.S.S.R. The *Jazz Singer* is the first motion picture with sound.

1928 Herbert Hoover is elected president. Congress approves $32 million to enforce prohibition. Hurricane sweeps Florida coast. Amelia Earhart is the first woman to fly across the Atlantic. The Lewis Meriam Survey publishes the shocking conditions of the Indian reservations. Chiang Kai-shek is elected president of China.

1929 U.S. stock market crashes, causing unemployment, worldwide depression, and business failures. The term "apartheid" is first used to describe South Africa's racial policies.

1930 More than 1,300 banks close due to stock market failure.

1931 Thomas Alva Edison dies. Wiley Post and Harold Getty are first to fly around the world. Earnest Lawrence invents the cyclotron, or "atom smasher." Gangster Al Capone is imprisoned for income tax evasion.

1932 Famine in the Soviet Union. Amelia Earhart becomes first woman to fly solo across the Atlantic Ocean. Franklin Delano Roosevelt wins landslide presidential victory.

1933 Charles Eastman is awarded the first Indian Achievement Award at the Chicago World's Fair. John Collier becomes Indian commissioner. Franklin Delano Roosevelt is inaugurated as the 32nd president. U.S. recognizes U.S.S.R. U.S. passes Twenty-first Amendment, which repeals prohibition. Adolf Hitler is appointed German chancellor. Japan withdraws from the League of Nations. Fulgencio Batista leads a *coup d'etat* in Cuba.

1934 Hitler is elected führer (leader) of Germany. U.S.S.R. joins League of Nations. Gandhi discontinues civil disobedience drive in India. The Wheeler-Howard Indian Reorganization Act overturns the Dawes Act. Total land owned by Indians totals just 47 million acres.

1935 American humorist Will Rogers dies in a plane crash. Amelia Earhart becomes the first woman to fly solo across the Pacific Ocean.

1936 "Stalin Constitution" is put into effect in U.S.S.R. Social security goes into effect in U.S. King Edward VIII abdicates the throne of Great Britain. Spanish Civil War begins.

1937 Amelia Earhart is lost on flight over Pacific Ocean. George VI is crowned king of Great Britain. Japan seizes Peking, Tientsin, and Shanghai.

1938 Germany annexes Austria. Bingo becomes a new rage and fund-raiser in U.S.

1939 Charles Eastman dies at the age of 80 in Detroit, Michigan. Hitler invades Poland, beginning World War II. Germany annexes Czechoslovakia. Soviet-Nazi nonaggression pact is signed. U.S.S.R. invades Finland. Spanish Civil War ends; Britain and France recognize Francisco Franco's new government in Spain.

INDEX—*Page numbers in boldface type indicate illustrations.*

107

108

ABOUT THE AUTHOR

Peter Anderson studied Native American literature and history while earning an M.A. in American Studies at the University of Wyoming. He has worked as a carpenter, editor, river guide, and newspaper reporter. Currently he lives in Salt Lake City where he teaches part-time and writes. During the summer, he is a wilderness ranger with the U.S. Forest Service.